HMEN

THE FILM COMPANION

PETER APERLO

TITAN BOOKS

WATCHMEN THE FILM COMPANION
Hardback 9781848561595
Paperback 9781848560673

Published by
Titan Books
A division of
Titan Publishing Group Ltd
144 Southwark St
London
SE1 0UP

First edition January 2009
10 9 8 7 6 5 4 3 2

Movie photography by Clay Enos.
Photo on page 170 by Dan Scudamore.

Visit our website: WWW.TITANBOOKS.COM

Did you enjoy this book? We love to hear from our readers.
Please e-mail us at: **readerfeedback@titanemail.com** or write to
Reader Feedback at the above address.

A CIP catalogue record for this title is available from the British Library.

Printed in the USA.

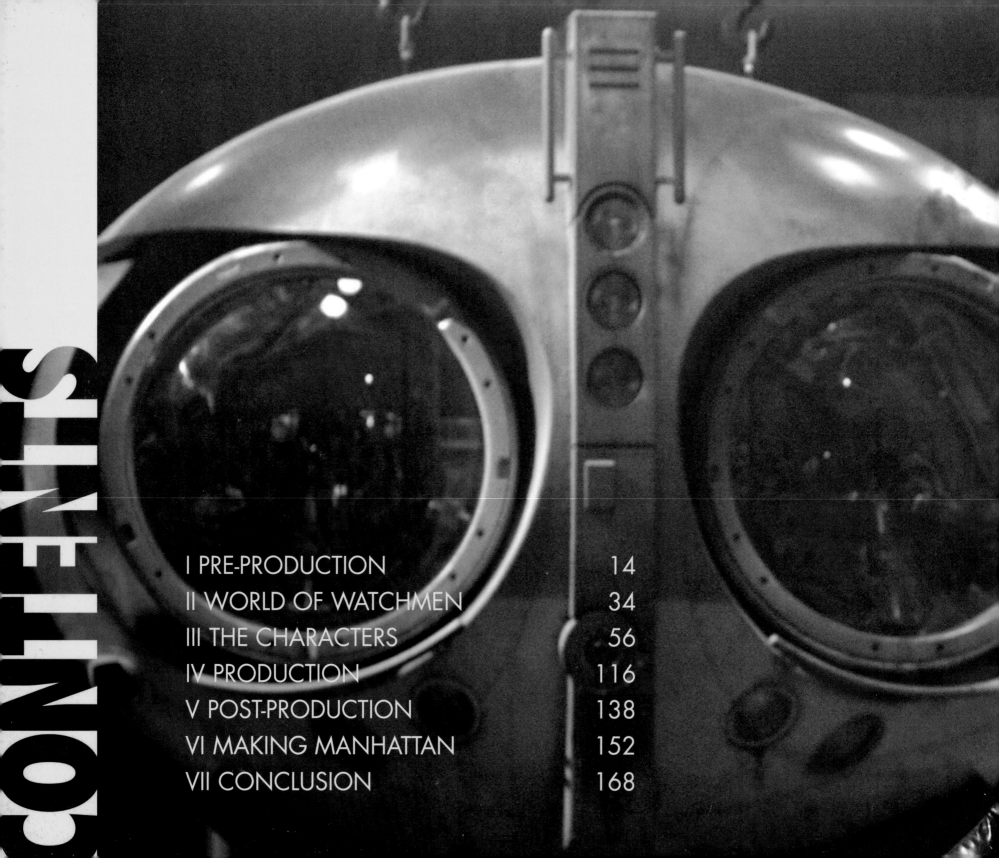

CONTENTS

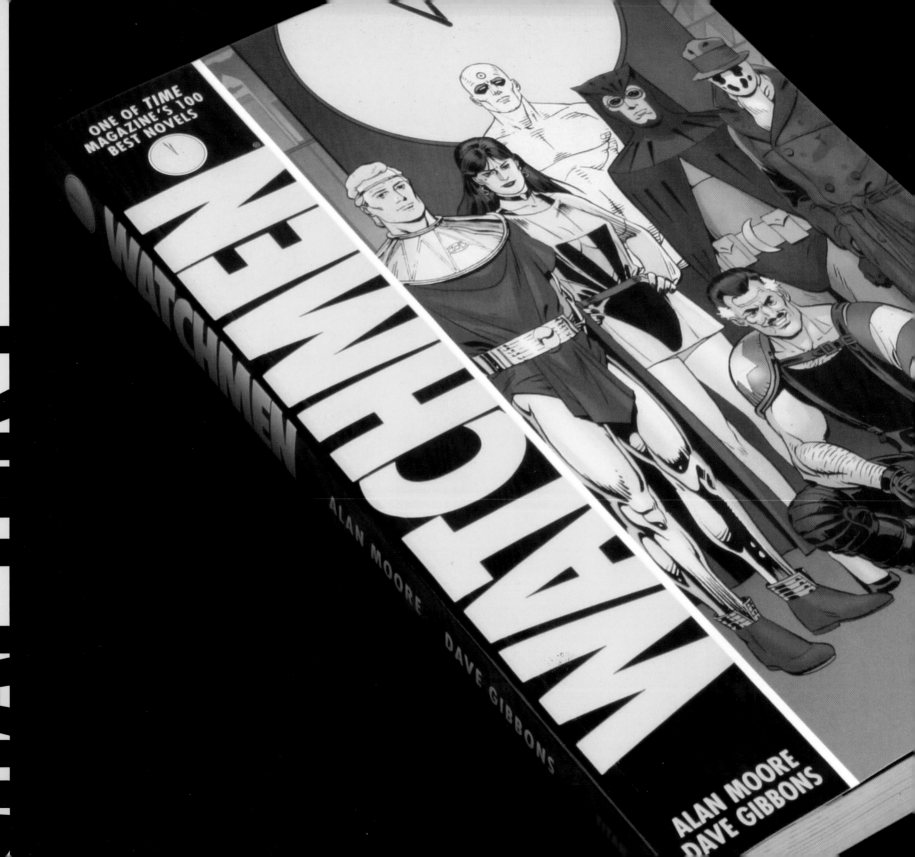

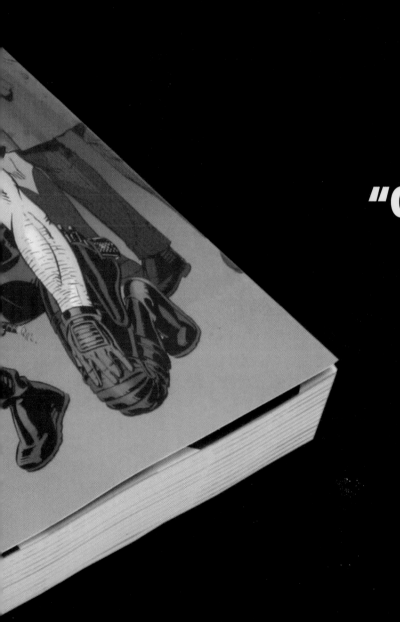

"QUIS CUSTODIET IPSOS CUSTODES."
– JUVENAL, *SATIRES*

GAZING INTO THE ABYSS

Watchmen is the most critically acclaimed graphic novel of all time. It captured a Hugo Award in 1988, and *Time Magazine* placed it among the "100 Best English-Language Novels From 1923 To The Present" in 2005 – the only graphic novel ever to achieve either distinction. These accolades came on top of winning the comic book industry's Jack Kirby Award for Best Writer/Artist Combination in 1987, an early indication that it was destined to become a classic. As a deconstruction and satire of the comic book super hero, this little twelve-issue series by Alan Moore and Dave Gibbons helped usher in a new era of maturity and sophistication to the genre.

Many people have taken stabs at developing this dense piece of work for the big screen; it was a bumpy twenty-year journey that began almost as soon as the original series was published. Despite a number of major studios being involved at one time or another and some well-known names being attached to direct and star, no one could ever get the project off the ground. Producer Larry Gordon explains, "In every way, *Watchmen* is anything but a typical studio movie. I'm thoroughly convinced it only got made because of Zack's involvement."

Early in pre-production, several comic book artists were invited to contribute conceptually to the film. Their work included these three takes on Nite Owl II, by Adam Hughes (left), David Finch (below left) and John Cassaday (right).

HOW DO OWL EYES WORK?

I'D LOVE TO REALLY SEE AN ORGANIC CENTRE TO THE LENS – LIKE AN ACTUAL OWL

Warner Bros. acquired the rights near the end of 2005. Enter director Zack Snyder. While he was eyeballs-deep in post-production on *300*, the film version of Frank Miller's passionate graphic novel about the Battle of Thermopylae, producers Larry Gordon and Lloyd Levin, along with upper brass at the studio, brought the project to Snyder to see if he was interested in helming *Watchmen*. Snyder was familiar with the work from reading it years before. "People are making a lot of graphic novels into movies, but *Watchmen*'s generally regarded as the touchstone work. It's the masterpiece," Snyder points out.

Having been offered the chance, Snyder felt he would bear some responsibility if a sub-par version got released, whether he was involved or not. It seemed a much better option to take some control of his own destiny. Thus began a months-long labor to convince the studio to let him film the story according to his vision – one that cleaved much closer to the original comic than the screenplays floating around at that time did. The financial success of *300* no doubt convinced the suits to trust Snyder's artistic judgment, and in the end they came around to his point of view.

Snyder and the producers collaborated with screenwriter Alex Tse on several rewrites that eventually restored the alternate-'80s setting, with Richard Nixon going on his fifth term in office and a nuclear exchange between the U.S. and the U.S.S.R. as a distinct possibility. Snyder wasn't concerned that this choice might relegate the film to being a period piece; he knew it contained enough universal themes to resonate strongly with the present. "When you take a medium and have it shine a light on humanity, that's what *Watchmen* does," says Snyder. "It's something to comment immediately on the pop culture of the moment, and at the same time it has this deep reflective quality that's timeless."

"MASK" is
A SILK SCARF!

Left: Nite Owl II re-imagined by David Finch. **Above:** Silk Spectre II as seen by Adam Hughes.

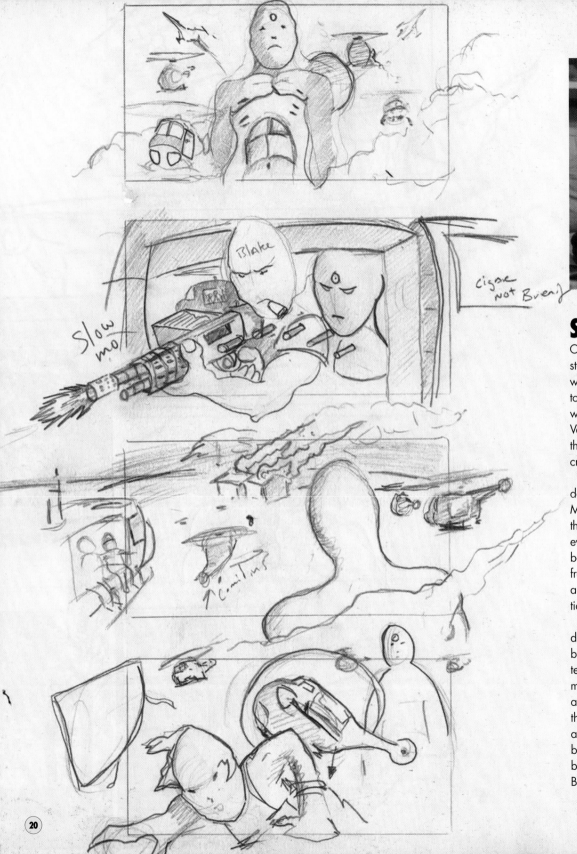

STORYBOARDS

Once the script was to his liking and the studio was onboard, Snyder started drawing. He drew until nearly six sketchbooks had been filled with storyboards detailing every angle of every shot from the WB logo to Rorschach's journal resting in the *New Frontiersman*'s crank file – as well as a complete work-up of a television commercial for Nostalgia by Veidt. The storyboards, along with the graphic novel, even more than the script, became the entry point for introducing potential cast and crewmembers to the project.

"The first thing that Zack did when we met in March 2007 was sit down and open his drawing books," says production designer Alex McDowell. "In the first few minutes of the meeting, we're going through the boards he had drawn – starting at the beginning, chronologically just every frame of the movie. That in itself was revelatory." Pasted in the books along with Snyder's drawings were countless picture references, from the graphic novel itself as well as photos from period magazines and newspapers – a testament to his profound desire to keep the production grounded in reality as well as being faithful to the source material.

A project with such an intricate narrative and visual density demanded thorough planning and coordination. Snyder's storyboards, as simple as they were, contained very specific instructions in terms of set construction, character blocking, costumes, and camera movements. "We pretty much set the script aside, since he had absorbed all the script stuff into the storyboards, and they were totally the Bible," says McDowell. Snyder looked at the boards as a guide, a necessary starting point for organizing such a design-heavy shoot – but never as a straitjacket. "The design of it happens a long time before we come to shoot it, and I change it on the day all the time. But I would say for the most part, we shoot what I drew," he explains.

TITLE SEQUENCE

Snyder's boards were particularly important for laying out the title credit sequence. This consisted of vignettes only mentioned briefly in the graphic novel or wholly invented for the film, but which were not explicitly presented in the script. This montage of alternate history was intended to force the audience to re-imagine the past by viewing it through a *Watchmen* lens. "The parallel universe has been set up so beautifully in the title sequence," McDowell says. "It really puts the audience square into a new kind of history. By the time you get to the end of it, even reading it on the storyboards, you start questioning, 'Which part of that was real again?'"

Producer Lloyd Levin explains, "Zack's title treatment very cleverly brings a lot of the book's texture of the film, while also providing the audience with an opportunity to get up to speed with the world of *Watchmen*."

The title sequence became a research project all its own. Recreating Kennedy's motorcade in Dallas, for example, involved digging deep into historical documents as well as conspiracy websites to dredge up such details as which cars were in what position, and the fact that Abraham Zapruder was being supported on his plinth by his secretary as he filmed the tragic event.

Opposite left: Zack Snyder's original storyboards for the Vietnam sequence. **Opposite right:** Snyder with Producer Larry Gordon.
Above Left: Concept art of Dr. Manhattan observing firsthand the Apollo moon landing.
Above: Producer Lloyd Levin on the New York set.

The New York Gazette

FINAL
★ ★ ★ ★ ★

NEW YORK, FRIDAY, NOVEMBER 1, 1985

VOL. CXXXV   No. 46,576   Copyright© 1985 The New York Gazette Company

★ ★ ★ | 30 cents beyond
New York City limits | 30

SOVIETS INVADE AFGHANISTAN

Stage Set for Genocide

By WILLIAM BALL
Special to The New York Gazette

WASHINGTON – The US and Britain had a quick response to the Soviet action taking place in Afghanistan. The White House called a Press Conference with President Nixon addressing the media on the question of military retaliation to the growing number of troops on the Afghanistan Pakistan border. The area know as the Frontier is a lawless stronghold of terrorism that cannot be tolerated. London backed President Nixon in his resolve to send troops to the region and urged the European powers to show solidarity in dealing with the Russian government. Relations with Russia were further complicated when the Pakistan government denied that support was building among the military Generals who have influence on the Tribal Leaders of the region.

well as a persistent challenge from Muslim fundamentalists.

Trying to keep Nixon out of the fray, his aides made no changes to his public appearances and Nixon is due to speak to the Congress the following day.

Senior US intelligence sources confirmed that Soviet troop movement has been building for weeks with tanks amassed in the major areas around Kabul and the Khyber Pass.

The Kremlin is denying the report and has issued a statement denouncing any involvement in the affairs of the Afghanistan government.

Krushev has not been seen in the public eye for quiet some time now and is rumored to be recovering from a bout of alcoholism in his dacha in the southern Georgia woods of the Ukraine. Tass has made mention in the Soviet pages of the

Lawless Stronghold of Terrorism

AThe US and Britain agreed that

TRACKING THE RUSSIANS

Some Defectors Join Afghan Rebels

By R. E. KLENGHOFFER
Special to The New York Gazette

WASHINGTON – The

This attention to even the smallest details – a quality seen in every frame of the graphic novel itself – infused all facets of production. "A lot of the time when I'm doing a film, the director's always pulling me back from going too far with the details," says McDowell. "The design department gets obsessive about, 'Oh, we want more, more, more,' and the director says, 'I'm never going to see it.' It's the classic mantra. But with Zack, it's, 'More, more, more, more!' because he's going to see all of it. He's going to feature the fine print in a newspaper article on the wall."

Add to those newspapers the dozens of framed photographs, the scores of trinkets and mementoes of past glories, and the countless advertisements and packaging for a whole host of consumer products – from canned beans, to hairspray, to Mmeltdowns. But could they really approach the same level of detail that's in *Watchmen*?

"That's a thing you just go, 'You know what? That's too huge a job for anyone to do,'" explains Snyder, "but when you're doing it shot by shot and moment by moment, it seems almost natural." Making it all happen was a gifted crew of designers and artisans who were or became rabid fans of the graphic novel and who felt free to suggest even more elements to include. The result of piling detail upon detail was a world that looked subtly different from our own, and yet felt utterly real. "It got to the point where I just expected the perfect bottle of fake cancer medicine or Veidt shoes. They did an amazing job," says Snyder. "That stuff is the thing that makes it such a complete world."

Opposite left: Veidt sport shoes on display in his office.

Opposite right: The iconic pirate comic brought to life, with cover by Dave Gibbons.

Above: The prop newspapers feature full-length articles.

CASTING

Snyder wanted to avoid movie stars in putting together his ensemble cast, feeling that their well-known personas might distract the audience from full immersion in the film's weighty narrative. He instead chose lesser known, but incredibly talented performers with the chops to completely embody their roles – people like Tony-Award-nominated Patrick Wilson and indie film veterans Carla Gugino and Billy Crudup. Internet postings by fans of the graphic novel pegged Jackie Earle Haley as the perfect Rorshach long before he returned to acting or got his Oscar nod for *Little Children*. He ended up actively campaigning for the role by submitting a video of himself as the masked vigilante, and it paid off. Any other actors playing those characters, and it would have been an

COSTUMES

Clothing those actors, as well as the throngs of extras, was another job entirely. The scope of the task was magnified by the fact that the story covered almost fifty years, many of these in brief flashbacks. The costumes needed to be spot on to convey an instantaneous sense of time and place to the viewer. Specialized costume house Quantum Creation FX provided the high-tech suits, such as those worn by Nite Owl II and Ozymandias. The rest were rented, bought, modified, or stitched completely by designer Michael Wilkinson's team. One challenge was trying to stay within the graphic novel's secondary color palette of greens, purples, and browns, while maintaining the desired realism. "The prison uniforms, for example, we really wanted to capture that murky grey/purple, so we bought raw pieces and had them dyed and adjusted to look like they do in the graphic novel," explains Wilkinson. He adds, "A lot of the police uniforms and things like that, we put an extra layer of grime and distressing on to make it feel like they had really been through the paces on the streets of New York."

SETS

Yet another way the filmmakers planned to reinforce the reality of the world was by having the actors interact in real environments whenever possible. One of the exceptions to this rule was, of course, the scenes taking place on Mars, which required extensive use of green screens and computer-generated images, much like Snyder's previous film, *300*. Still, they intended to shoot the majority of *Watchmen* on physical sets, almost all of which needed to be built from the ground up.

Despite the costs involved, the producers gradually understood the reasoning. "It became obvious that we basically had to build everything and create the environments," recalls executive producer Herb Gains, "which is what we did." McDowell, who had designed sets for such diverse productions as *Fight Club*, *Minority Report*, and *Charlie and the Chocolate Factory*, admits to never having to build as much as he did on *Watchmen*.

After considering such far-flung locales as Australia, Spain, Eastern Europe, London, and even New York City itself, Snyder and company settled on Vancouver, British Columbia as the spot that offered the best mix of adaptable locations and the required breadth of talent. In the summer of 2007, an army of builders descended on the town. Over the course of the shoot, their labors would eventually produce over 150 sets on four soundstages – sets ranging from the great hall at Karnak to the Owl Chamber – not to mention the conversion of an abandoned paper mill into both Dr. Manhattan's laboratory and Sing Sing Prison. Of course, the most Herculean task before them was the construction of New York City.

NEW YORK

The original plan had been to shoot on one of the "New York Streets" available in several studio backlots in Southern California. Traditional backlots, however, have streets that end in a "T" in order to contain the frame and give the illusion that the streets continue off into the rest of the unseen city. Nowadays, CG technology being what it is, a better solution is to build entirely new streets that end abruptly in blue screens; later, artists can digitally paint in a much more realistic-looking cityscape beyond that, extending to the horizon. They can also digitally extend the buildings vertically into skyscrapers.

That is why they ended up transforming a lumberyard in Burnaby, B.C. into three blocks of midtown Manhattan – with a little Saigon thrown in for good measure. This mammoth construction project consumed over 200,000 nails, 10,000 sixteen-foot 2x4s, and 384,000 square feet of foam brick. Contained within this fourteen-acre backlot were Dan's brownstone, Moloch's rat-hole, and the Comedian's high-rise. Treasure Island Comics sat across the street from a certain newsstand, just a block away from the Gunga Diner. Many portions were much more than mere facades, and contained filmable interiors.

After basic construction was complete, McDowell, Oscar-nominated set decorator Jim Erickson, and their crew spent weeks laboring to make the city look "lived in." The buildings received successive layers of paint, graffiti, and posters, in addition to an overall weathering process (aided by the ample local "liquid sunshine"), to give them just the right amount of near-apocalyptic neglect.

Previous spread right: The Owl Chamber.

This spread and next spread: Views of the gritty New York set.

The script also called for a practical set that the crew dubbed the "Creepy House," as it was to be the macabre home of the child moles-ter that Rorschach tracks down. Initial location scouting had turned up a squalid former crack house that could serve, but a follow-up visit by Snyder, McDowell, and others found within it freakish parallels almost beyond imagining. Beside the bizarre mix of dilapidated wallpaper, paint, and paneling used to "decorate" the interior, an old picture of a pirate ship hung crookedly from one wall. All the kitchen cabinets had been installed upside down, unsettlingly placing the handles in awk-ward positions. But most disturbing of all was the fact that the site – just like in the graphic novel – was the lair of two large, free-roaming dogs, whose feces littered the floor and yard.

Hygiene concerns rendered the location unusable, but careful meas-urements were taken and the house was re-created on the backlot – this time with fake dog poop. This just goes to show that you can't control where you'll find inspiration, especially when tackling a project of this complexity, but you take what you can get. "Those accidents drive you to a place you couldn't imagine," says McDowell.

This page and opposite left: The "Creepy House" set, inside and out.

NORAD

Another peculiar coincidence occurred when director of photography Larry Fong was showing his gaffer and key grip some of the concept art and photo references just after hiring them. Coming to pictures of the war room from *Dr. Strangelove*, which they really wanted to emulate for the scenes of Nixon at NORAD, Fong says, "I told the gaffer, 'You know, we can't figure out how they made these images on the walls up there. I'm saying it's projection, and they're saying it's painted graphics with light bulbs.' And he goes, 'Oh, I know how they did that. That was rear projection.' And I said, 'Well, how do you know that?' And he goes, 'Because I was there. I was doing the rear projection.' 'Well, I'm glad I hired you.' That's crazy. What's the chance of that?"

"The thing that's been interesting about this film across the board," says McDowell, "has been the overlap between fact and fiction. Even more than the graphic novel, Zack has pulled it to this pop culture reference point with the full knowledge that this audience knows so much about contemporary pop culture in a way that not even Alan Moore and Dave Gibbons knew at the time – putting Nixon in Kubrick's war room, that kind of mélange." And those are the kinds of things *Watchmen* absolutely revels in.

Above: The NORAD war room set, inspired by *Dr. Strangelove*.

CHAPTER II

"A BIG THEME IN *WATCHMEN* IS NOSTALGIA, LONGING FOR A SIMPLER TIME..."
– ZACK SNYDER

WORLD OF WATCHMEN

America never went in much for super heroes – not in comic books, anyway. And she got tired of the real ones soon enough, but not before they changed the world in unimaginable ways. At least, that's how it is in the alternate universe where *Watchmen* takes place. Just like in our world, the June 1938 debut issue of *Action Comics* introduced a certain super-powered refugee from a doomed planet wearing blue and red tights and a flapping cape while he fought for Truth, Justice, and the American Way. This other-worldly savior possessed an unwavering moral compass to match his great strength, which some found reassuring as the globe sparked and sputtered into the conflagration that was World War II.

But the Man of Steel, and other comic book heroes like him, drifted into the background and were forgotten as flesh-and-blood costumed vigilantes began showing up in newspapers and newsreels across the country. They were a natural foil to the crooks that had taken to wearing Halloween get-ups to avoid identification. "They don't have super-hero comics in this world because super heroes are an everyday occurrence," explains Zack Snyder. "Why would you make a comic book about it? It's not adventure. It's not exotic anymore." By the early '60s, if you mentioned the term 'superman' to the average person, it conjured up the image of an entirely different being. But more on him later.

•Watchmen History   •World History   •Alternate World History
>Indicates a scripted event

THE WATCHMEN (aka The Minutemen)

1. THE COMEDIAN (Edward Blake) b.1918
2. NITE OWL 1 (Hollis Mason) b.1917
3. SILK SPECTRE 1 (Sally Jupiter) b.1918
4. MOTHMAN
5. SILHOUETTE
6. DOLLAR BILL
7. CAPTAIN METROPOLIS
8. HOODED JUSTICE (Omitted)

THE NEW WATCHMEN (aka The Crimebusters)

1. THE COMEDIAN (Edward Blake)
2. NITE OWL 2 (Dan Dreiberg) b.1950
3. SILK SPECTRE 2 (Laurie Juspeczyk) b.1953
4. DR. MANHATTAN (Jon Osterman) b.1930
5. OZYMANDIAS (Adrian Veidt) b.1950
6. RORSCHACH (Walter Kovacs) b.1942
7. CAPTAIN METROPOLIS

FRIENDS

JANEY SLATER (Dr. M's girlfriend) b.1933
WALLY WEAVER (Dr. M's work colleague)

1930s

US Flag, 48 stars
Est'd 1912

>5p1: **Nite Owl 1** (20) fights at Opera House

>5p5: **Comedian** (21) takes out bank robber
>5p3: **Sally Jupiter** (21) photo w/ Police Chief
WWII begins

3 Doomsday Clock

1940s

>5p6/7,10p,12p,34p,45p: **The Watchmen** group photo
>34p: **Comedian(Blake)** (22) assaults **Sally** (22)
Hollis (23) to the rescue

USA enters WWII

'42 >5p8: Norman Rockwell paints **Sally Jupiter (Silk Spectre)** (24) with Hitler

'44 D-Day - June 06

>5p9/10/12/13pt: **Comedian (Blake)** (27) lands at Iwo Jima, plants flag
>5p17/18/19: **Silhouette** kisses girlfriend
>124pt: **Nite Owl 1** (28) fights villains
>5p15/16: Einstein cries at bomb screening
>65p9: **Jon** (15) learns watch repair from his father
Iwo Jima flag raising - Feb 23
VJ Day - Aug 14
US Drops Atomic Bombs on Hiroshima and Nagasaki - Aug 06, 09

'46

'47 7 Doomsday Clock Invented

1950s

'50 >5p25/26: Young **Kovacs (Rorschach)** (8) sees man pay his mother
>80pt: Young **Kovacs (Rorschach)** (8) spit upon

'51 >5p21: **Dollar Bill** is shot during bank heist

'52

'53 2
>5p23: **Sally Jupiter** (35) retires, pregnant
>5p22: **Mothman** to asylum in ambulance

'54 >5p24: **Silhouette** & her girlfriend found dead in her apartment
The Watchmen disband
>5p27: **Hollis** (37) & **Comedian** (36) pack up

'55

'56

'57 >5p42: Kruschev announces Sputnik 2 w/ Laika, the dog, going into space

'58

'59 US Flag, 49 stars
Est'd 1959
>65p6: **Jon** (29) meets Janey (26) for the first time in a bar
>65p2/4: **Jon** & Janey go on Carnival date

1960s

'60 US Flag, 50 stars 7
Est'd 1960

>65p5/7/8/10: **Jon Osterman (30)** in Reactor Chamber
>65p11/12/14/16/18: **Jon** materializes in Cafeteria, & outside by fence
>65pt: **Dr. Manhattan** introduced to world
>5p28/29: **Dr M** neutralizes tank
>5p35/36/37: Televised Nixon-Kennedy debates - Sep
>5p34: Kruschev pounding table at UN - Oct

>2pb: **Dr M** stops warheads in flight
Bay of Pigs
Berlin Wall built

'62 >5p38: **Dr M** shakes hands w/ JFK
Cuban Missile Crisis

>5p39/40/41: President Kennedy assassinated, **The Comedian** (45) is the shooter

'64 >5p49: Kruschev & Castro watch ICBM's go by
>65p26: **Dr M**, explodes mobsters head

>65p30: **Dr M & Janey** (33), Christmas, he turns her tear to a diamond
US sends troops to Vietnam

'66 >5p43/44/45: **Laurie Juspeczyk** (13) watches TV with her parents (Vietnamese monk sets himself on fire)
>27,136: Laurie sees her parents argue

Hollis' memoirs, "Under the Hood" published

'68

>5p48: Nixon sworn in - Jan
>5p54/55,69: Apollo Moon Landing - Jul

1970s

'70 >5p58,10p,45p: **New Watchmen** photo
>38,62p,65p31: First meeting of **The New Watchmen**
Laurie's (17) debut as **Silk Spectre**
>38,65p31: **Laurie** (17) meets **Dr M**, Janey (37) angry
>63p: **Laurie** talks to the **Comedian** (52)
>5p50/51/52: Vietnam war protest

>35: **Comedian** (53) **and Dr M** meet in Vietnam
>35,65p25: **Dr M**, 100 ft tall in Vietnam
>45pt: **Comedian** w/ flamethrower
>65p21: **Dr M** causes Viet Cong surrender
>36: **Comedian** confronted in Saigon bar by pregnant woman
>36: Comedian gets facial scar
>65p20: **Dr M** turns warhead into leaves

'72 Nixon begins 2nd term
Woodward & Bernstein found dead during Watergate investigation
>7p: Blake (Comedian) (55) Shakes hands with Nixon (Still Photo)

'74 >5p46/47: Two criminals tied to a hydrant; Rorschach calling card on ground

'75 >5p53: **Nite Owl 1**, Warhol portrait
>80-87: Rorschach (33) kills child molester

'76 >65p56: **Ozymandias (Veidt)** outside Studio 54

'77 US Flag, 51 stars 7
Est'd 1977
>5p61: TV wall - Protesters "Badges not Masks"; Dick Cavett Show; Doomsday clock
>5p61: Nixon at podium
>5p61: Keene Act passed (no masked heroes)
>5p61: Vietnam named 51st state
>40: **Nite Owl 2** (27) **& Comedian** (59) control Anti-vigilante crowds
Nixon begins 3rd term - Jan

'78 >65p22/28: Wally Weaver's interview
>65p24: Hollis' (63) interview for his book "Dawn of the Superhero"
>149pt: **Veidt** (29) poisons Wally & Janey (46) at Pyramid Industries

1980s

'80

'81 >65p3: Wally Weaver dies of cancer
Nixon begins 4th term

'82

'83

'84

'85 Nixon begins 5th term
OCTOBER 12, 1985
5 >2pb: Doomsday Clock

>**The Comedian** (67) is murdered

OUR STORY BEGINS....

REVISED Nov 27, 2007
B. Wilson

The earliest costumed heroes were not people with incredible powers, but they were endowed with extraordinary motivations. Hollis Mason, although he was not the first, was genuinely inspired by Superman's example to battle for extralegal justice; the reasons others had for dressing up and fighting crime were as many and as varied as the garish costumes they wore. Some were bored and wanted the excitement. Some were poor and wanted the publicity. Some simply got off on it – in every way imaginable.

Snyder points out that one of the fundamental questions *Watchmen* asks is, "Who is a super hero? What is it about this certain individual that made him choose being a super hero? It might seem like an obvious lifestyle choice for some people, but on the other hand, you give up a lot. You give up your privacy, your ability to have a normal relationship, your ability to have a normal job – all the things that we take for granted."

The flip side is living with the consequences of that choice. "What does that do to you?" Snyder asks, echoing some of the themes explored in the graphic novel and the film. "Does it make you crazy? Does it make you a recluse? Does it make you lose touch with humanity?"

Previous spread left: Nite Owl I foils an attempted mugging.
Previous spread right: A timeline helped cast and crew keep track of how times have changed.

Left: Sally Jupiter poses for a war bond poster.
Right: The glory days of the Minutemen captured for posterity.

MINUTEMEN

In 1939, the costumed vigilantes in New York City organized themselves into a group they called the Minutemen. Latter-day critics have leveled the accusation that they were simply performing street theater while unspeakable atrocities were being committed on the far sides of the Atlantic and Pacific, but the American Public loved it. The Minutemen became instant celebrities, personages to be gabbed about in gossip columns. Some of them sought out this spotlight, while others shunned it.

They took out scores of bad guys in eccentric attire throughout the '40s, but strong personalities, gigantic egos, and flawed humans made for tricky collaboration. Sally Jupiter's agent, in charge of publicity for the Minutemen, became quite deft at sweeping their more scandalous deeds under the rug – things like fascist and racist remarks, sexual assaults, and homosexual love affairs (both open and closeted).

Above: A B-29 bomber with distinctive nose art flattens Hiroshima.
Below: Villains from the Minutemen's past.

Opposite: Eddie Blake finds Sally irresistible, but Hooded Justice isn't having it.

Below: Sally Jupiter hangs up her costume after one last supper.

But these were not what ultimately brought the team down. By the time the '50s rolled around, all the interesting crooks were behind bars, dead, reformed, or had moved on to sneakier crimes that were resistant to the direct fisticuffs approach. Some of the heroes themselves had died or had begun to show signs of mental instability. Sally retired to raise her daughter. In the maelstrom of McCarthyism and Red paranoia, Hooded Justice disappeared after refusing to testify before Congress.

Costumed heroes also started to feel a little stupid when they stepped out in public to fight criminals dressed in civvies. The Minutemen disbanded in 1954, although a dedicated few soldiered on as individuals into the next decade. The first wave was definitely over.

The lifestyle, however, was not. What had been just another crazy fad became a concept entrenched in the American psyche: it was a given that some people would take the law into their own hands, and authorities would simply look the other way.

Above: Dollar Bill rues the decision to wear a cape.
Below: Mothman finds the stress too much for him.

With the coming of the 'New Frontier' of the '60s, a younger generation of vigilantes emerged. An adventurer rumored to be the world's smartest man used his wits and precisely honed body to crush drug syndicates. A young man took up the mantle of the elder Nite Owl and fought crime with a dazzling array of gadgetry. Another, his face hidden behind a mask of ever-shifting inkblots, doggedly tracked criminals to their lairs to exact righteous vengeance. Even Sally Jupiter's little girl, with her mother's heavy-handed encouragement, was getting into the act.

The newcomer who made the whole world sit up and take notice, however, was Dr. Manhattan. The result of physicist Jon Osterman's suffering a horrendous nuclear accident at a U.S. Government laboratory, he was able to perceive and manipulate matter on a molecular scale, teleport virtually anywhere instantaneously, and was for all intents and purposes indestructible. His appearance in 1959 was a signal that things would never be the same.

Dr. Manhattan's existence posed a terrifying conundrum, one that Snyder finds intriguing. Especially critical is the way the super-being affected the *Watchmen* world. "He's one of my favorite characters because he does bring into question so many things about our own way of thinking," he says, pointing out that, "When you see a Superman movie or a movie where there's a hero with super powers, no one ever

creature who has to share the planet with him. What does it mean to religion? What does it mean to politics? What does it mean to all things you interact with? Dr. Manhattan represents, like the atomic bomb, this ability to save us and destroy us at the same moment."

Dr. Manhattan eventually supplanted nuclear weapons as the lynchpin of America's national defense. He started out with public demonstrations of his power, and then dabbled in fighting crime. Things changed in earnest when he won the Vietnam War essentially singlehandedly. That stunning success earned a long stay in office for the man who was bold enough to ask him to do it, President Richard Nixon. (The Comedian's covert activities didn't hurt his presidency, either.)

Dr. Manhattan's abilities also allowed research in many areas such as genetics and materials to advance in leaps and bounds. As of 1985, he was collaborating with Adrian Veidt on a cheap, renewable form of power based on his own energy pattern to replace fossil fuels.

All those triumphs, however, were apt to leave some people feeling insecure. At the top of that list were the Soviets. There was no détente between Washington and Moscow after Vietnam, as in our timeline. The doctrine of "Mutually Assured Destruction" (MAD) no longer applied when one side essentially had a god in its corner. The nuclear arms race spiraled out of control as the Russians stockpiled tens of thousands of missiles in an attempt to present a viable counter to the threat posed to

Previous spread: Blake's amorality is matched only by Dr. Manhattan's apathy.

Opposite: Dr. Manhattan's existence alters history and the balance of power.

Above: In his fifth term, President Nixon consults with his top advisors in

Geneva Talks, U.S. Refuses to Discuss Dr. Manhattan

By WILLIAM BALL
Special to The New York Gazette

GENEVA, SWITZERLAND - President Nixon and Soviet Premier Mikhail Gorbachev met in Geneva for three days this week to talk about peace, international diplomatic relations and the arms race. President Nixon called the meeting in response to the tense atmosphere between the two superpowers and the ticking metaphorical Doomsday Clock, which is reportedly at 5 minutes to midnight.

In their meeting, Gorbachev and his foreign minister demanded to know more about the US's intentions for Dr. Manhattan, or what the soviets call "the Unfair Advantage" or "The Living Weapon". Nixon refused to divulge any information regarding Dr. Manhattan, the atomically altered scientist who has fought for the US in previous wars. He only said, "Dr. Manhattan is a scientist and continues to work as a scientist".

After the summit, Gorbachev said in a comment to the press, "We viewed the Geneva meeting realistically, without grand expectations, yet we hoped to lay the foundations for a serious dialogue in the future. However, if

President Nixon is unwilling to discuss, what the world knows to be, the biggest threat to the safety and future of the planet, should it go unchecked, then the roots for a serious problem grow".

US Foreign Analyst, Professor Blake William PhD. is concerned that this Geneva talk has done more harm than good. "Our President called the summit promising peace talks and giving the illusion of transparency. However, I believe his refusal to discuss what the rest of the world thinks is the most pressing topic, shows that we are hiding something".

It still seems too early to tell what effect the summit has had on the Soviet leaders. While Americans wait, The White House has declined offers to release a comment with their review of the summit.

William worries that the longer The White House declines comment, the more fear and unrest will show up on the streets in America. Americans need answers too. Poor leadership creates mistrust and revolt.

It was former president Eisenhower who championed the great need for world leaders to have personal relationships in order to

Continued on Page Two, Column 5

Group Fights to Preserve Civil Rights

By WILLIAM BALL
Special to The New York Gazette

NEW YORK - Stunts performed by men around town, in the last month, were originally thought to be the work of members of the crime-fighting group commonly known as the Watchmen. Now, another group has admitted to being responsible for the costumed stunts.

Fathers 4 Family Peace, a civil rights group, interrupted a National Lottery Draw live off air on NBC in front of ten million viewers last night in their most recent stunt. Group members appeared in their own broadcast in full super-hero costume to deliver their message.

"Now That We Have your Attention, We Ask for your Support"

Their leader, a man who did not identify himself and who was wearing a bat costume, said that they were a group of fathers fighting for justice and equality in the family courts. Their daytime activities include lobbying, petition writing and some communications

automatically granting custody to mothers in divorce cases. Now they are trying to draw more attention to the issue by raising public curiosity with costumed stunts.

"Now that we have your attention, we ask for your support. Everyone knows a divorced or divorcing couple with children. What most people don't realize is that there is great injustice and also a blind decision making process in the granting of custody for children," said the leader in his statement.

Before NBC was able to regain control of their channel the bat costumed man was able to elucidate. "Parents are not evaluated by the court or by psychiatric professionals. When mothers are automatically given full custody of the couple's children based solely on the fact the women have traditionally been our society's child caregivers, there is no evaluation of the mother to determine her suitability for care-taking".

"Oftentimes, one parent or the other has a substance or other problem

The New York Gazette

RICHARD FULBRIGHT, *Publisher*
DOUGLAS GARDNER, *Executive Editor*
ALLEN WYNDER, *Managing Editor*
EDGAR L. RAY, *Deputy Managing Editor*
JOHN WIKERSON, *Assistant Managing Editor*

ANGELA FRENCH, *Editorial Page Editor*
STEPHEN RICH, *Deputy Editorial Page Editor*
VERONICA LEWIS, *Exec. V.P., General Manager*
E. J. HORNIG, *Exec. V.P., General Manager*
ALVIN MEYER, *Assistant Managing Editor*

Who Do They Think They Are?

For any citizen who has been watching the newsstands over this last, unbearable month, there can be little doubt who I am referring to. In the current edition of pseudo-intellectual Marxist-brat-rock-star monthly Nova Express, cocaine-advocating editor DOUGLAS ROTH makes a vitriolic and unfounded attack upon the tradition of the masked lawman in our culture and attempts to stir up old prejudices and hatreds into a bloody wave of civil disorder.

It is hardly necessary

serve mankind? And if those laws through unforeseen circumstance become no longer applicable, is it not more noble to follow the course of right and justice; to serve the spirit of the law rather than its every dot and comma? In my book, anyone answering that question in the negative is someone without the moral backbone necessary to call himself an American. In the case of the Nova Express articles and their perpetrators, I would go so far as to call such a denial of time-tested patriotic virtues as being most definitely ANTI-American.

COKED-OUT COMMIE COWARDS

and Our

d of mine try to obtain I have been faced with our justice system and playing a case in order

friend, I also have an se lawyer who used to his observations to you. my experience and from introducing him to various friend was accused of has confessed that he is

admit guilt and hope that who has made a mistake d fit the crime?" he asked

elieves that most people sometimes make mistakes. ecause the justice system, to be innocent until proven ayed so that the accused shed for fear of worse

its, defense attorney's and a case. ecomes an toss up between expensive lawyer well versed

The fear of thermonuclear annihilation that had previously merely punctuated moments of the early Cold War, now had cemented itself into a permanent, numbing malaise as the populace adjusted to living under a whole ceiling-full of Swords of Damocles. One of the ways this sense of foreboding manifested itself was in the general neglect people paid to their environment. Buildings were run down, surrounded by trash and covered in layer upon layer of weathered posters and graffiti scrawls. Nobody seemed to be buying new cars with war a constant blip on the edge of the radar screen. Late '60s/early '70s models were the most common vehicles on the streets, even in 1985.

This spread: Crime-busting begins to seem a bit irrelevant as the Cold War heats up.

Next spread left: Nite Owl II and Rorschach make an effective team even after the failure of the Watchmen.
Next spread right: Veidt explores other pursuits.

Weather
Sunny and cool today, increasing cloudiness tonight. Tomorrow mostly cloudy with a chance of rain. Details page 24.

The New York Gazette

FINAL
★★★★★

NEW YORK, THURSDAY, JUNE 18, 1970

VOL. CXIX   No. 40,925   Copyright © 1970 The New York Gazette Company

★★★   10 CEN

SOVIETS CALL DR. M.
'IMPERIALIST WEAPON

President Nixon Responds with Public Statement

By ALLEN WYNDER
Special to The New York Gazette

WASHINGTON - President Nixon has responded to the Soviet slander, which called our Dr. Manhattan an imperialist weapon last week, with a televised public statement. The statement denounces the Soviet claims, defends Dr. Manhattan's actions and calls Russian foreign policy the perfect example of Imperialism.

President Nixon said, "Dr. Manhattan only has peace in mind. He was a physics scientist through and through and has the interests of the world through peace and science in mind. The fact that he has super-human powers only amplifies the need for him to do his part because he has the ability."

The soviets specifically called for Dr. Manhattan to leave Vietnam saying that "the Americans are not fighting a war but simply taking over a country with extreme force". Additionally, they accused Dr. Manhattan as being just one aspect of a multi-tiered imperialist plan, with oil

thieving, corrupt core of the military monopoly, which is the main monopoly support base for ultra-right and fascist movements, both here in the U.S. and world-wide.

President Nixon also said, "Dr. Manhattan is not part of any plan. He operates of his own free will according to his values as an American and as a scientist." In response to the armaments sales accusations, the President had no comment other than to say, "The USA has various alliances with different countries. Just as it has for years. Just like the rest of the world has. To divulge our ally secrets would be silly."

The Pentagon and Arms Dealers are Pushing this Secrecy Policy

Locksmith and McDonald Dennahead, along with the Pentagon and arms dealers, are pushing this secrecy policy. What they won't tell you though is that the weapons sales to countries surrounding Vietnam are related to the policy of exploitation and imperialism's profits - more guns, more profits.

Russia also claimed that Dr. Manhattan's force

choice will be picked by the U.S. corporations that have property in these countries. The arms will be sold to countries where U.S. corporations have the largest holdings.

The arms will be sold to countries with the most reactionary governments. U.S. imperialism wants to arm the countries that can be used in the aggression against North Vietnam. U.S. imperialism will sell arms to countries that will use them against their own working class.

The President Reassures the American People

Our President closed by reassuring the American people that, "whatever the Soviets say or think, is

Continued on Page Two, Column 5

Dr. Manhattan has been listed as a threat to Soviets.

Soviet Foreign Minister Andrei Gromyko declares that his government is very upset over US domination, declaring Dr. Manhattan as a secret weapon. Diplomatic channels have cooled between the super powers. The White House has yet to respond.

RUSSIA
DEMAN
WORL
INQUI

Soviets A
Investiga
Into Origins

By E. J. H
Special to The Ne

MOSCOW
Secretary
Communist
Soviet Uni
Brezhnev dem
to a go
investigation
of Dr. Manhat
less than a
reportedly
idea by sayi
into "a po

The m
seeks to pla
the US atte
ruled out a
the super
saying that
have the m
th mat
officials
repeatedly
campaign
part of
internati
U.S.
Secretar
said Frid
didn't h
anything
to," he con

NARCOTICS EDUCATION PROGRAM NOW

Drug Use Amongst

Senator Refutes Claims of Money Mismanagement

By VERONICA LEWIS
Special to The New York Gazette

over the top," he described. But the senator's office is not just spending

Some people insisted that this same board be loaned bond money to bail the district out. How could

FAMILY OF SIX KILLED IN HOME FIRE

Two Children Away

NEW FRONTIERSMAN

★★★★

HONOR IS LIKE THE HAWK: SOMETIMES IT MUST GO HOODEI

Hector Godfrey, Editor

RED ARMAGEDDON!

In this, the eleventh hour, with the world poised on the brink of Red Armageddon, it is vital that we, as a nation, should rally around those symbols that are closest to the great, warm, red-white-and-blue beating heart of this beleaguered country. They are our hope and our inspiration, the legends that urge our people onward even in times of deepest crisis.

Would our sense of national identity, our pride, our sens would these things be so enduring were it not for such great of freedom as Paul Revere's midnight ride, or the Alamo, or Gettysburg address? I think not. And yet, it seems that ther who, even in the dire adversity that besets us, see fit to ri deride the very notions that have made America what sh

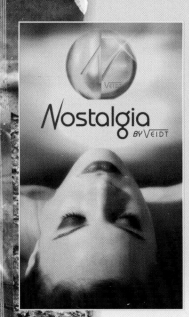

OZYMANDIAS

African Famine Relief

JOIN IN THE FIGHT AGAINST HUNGER

YANKEE STADIUM·NEW YORK

July 12, 1984

NOSTALGIA

Constant nuclear peril also had an effect on advertising and marketing. Some ads, like those for the fruity candy Mmeltdowns, overtly referenced the threat and turned it into a dark joke. Others, such as the retro-sensual commercials for Veidt's Nostalgia cologne, pulled the viewer into the classier, more carefree world of yesteryear. "A big theme in *Watchmen* is nostalgia, longing for a simpler time and things of that nature," says Snyder. "But it's interesting when you examine those simpler times, there was some dark thing in them. It's never as easy as remembering."

Another group that felt redundant and replaced by the arrival of Dr. Manhattan and the resurgence of costumed vigilantes was the police. They had to sit by and watch civilians in crazy outfits grab the glory and the headlines while the poorly paid flatfoots got no recognition for doing the same job – and those masks didn't have anyone peeking over *their* shoulders and making sure *they* followed the rules!

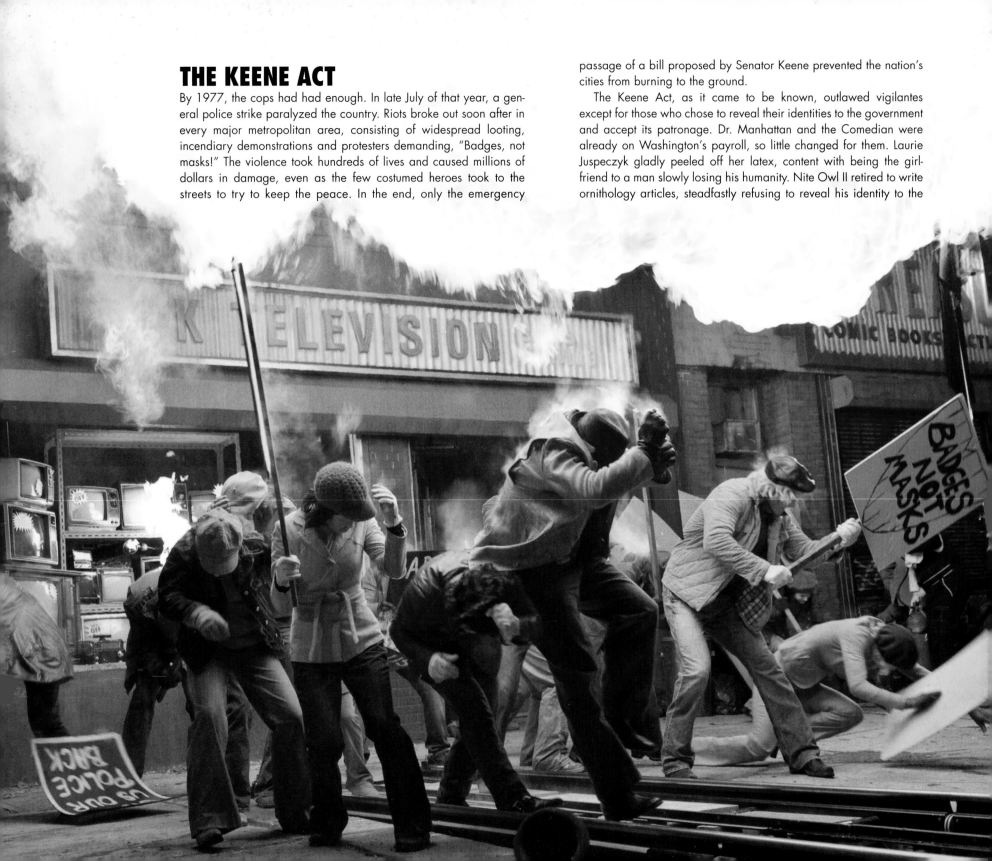

THE KEENE ACT

By 1977, the cops had had enough. In late July of that year, a general police strike paralyzed the country. Riots broke out soon after in every major metropolitan area, consisting of widespread looting, incendiary demonstrations and protesters demanding, "Badges, not masks!" The violence took hundreds of lives and caused millions of dollars in damage, even as the few costumed heroes took to the streets to try to keep the peace. In the end, only the emergency passage of a bill proposed by Senator Keene prevented the nation's cities from burning to the ground.

The Keene Act, as it came to be known, outlawed vigilantes except for those who chose to reveal their identities to the government and accept its patronage. Dr. Manhattan and the Comedian were already on Washington's payroll, so little changed for them. Laurie Juspeczyk gladly peeled off her latex, content with being the girl-friend to a man slowly losing his humanity. Nite Owl II retired to write ornithology articles, steadfastly refusing to reveal his identity to the authorities. That left only Rorschach as the lone mask and a fugitive from justice.

Adrian Veidt, perhaps sensing the way the wind was blowing, had much earlier given up adventuring and made it public that he was Ozymandias. That failed meeting in 1970, when he had tried to organize the Watchmen into a crime-fighting league, showed him that he needed to think much bigger to cure the world's ills. That led him to building up the Veidt Enterprises business empire to fund his research – all in the service of a hideous plan of unspeakable proportions.

Previous spread: Chaos erupts as the police go on strike to protest costumed heroes.

This spread: Nite Owl II witnesses the American Dream disappearing before his eyes.

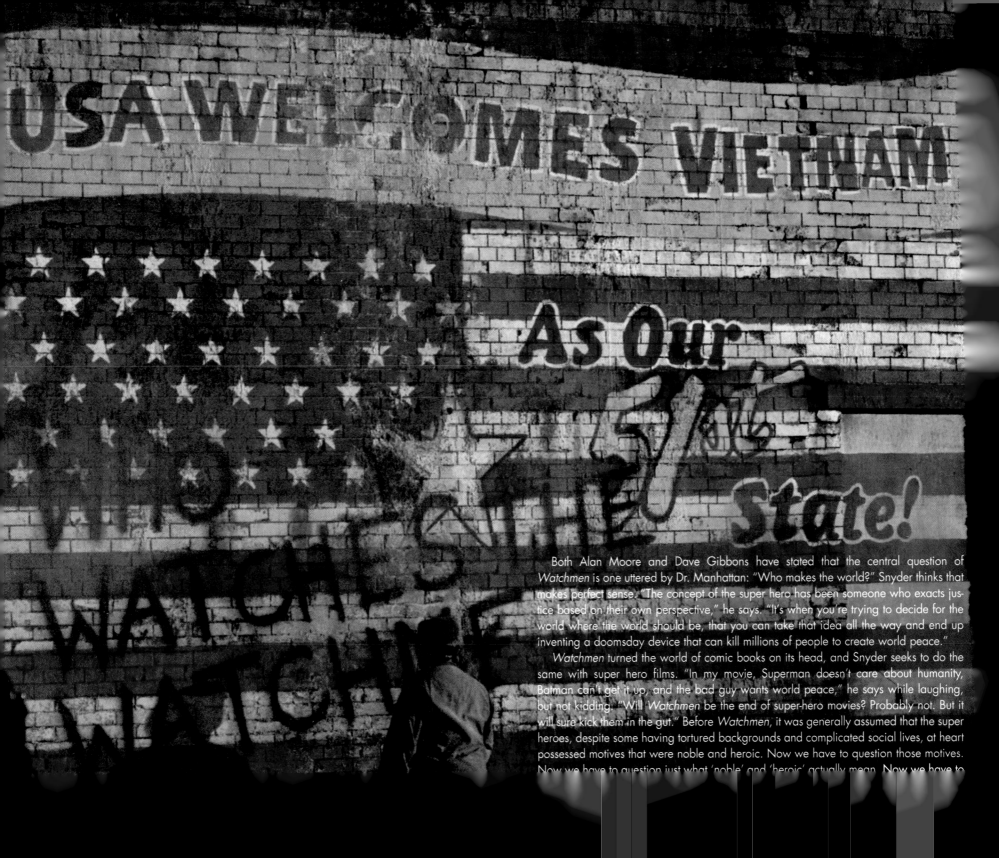

USA WELCOMES VIETNAM

As Our 51st State!

Both Alan Moore and Dave Gibbons have stated that the central question of *Watchmen* is one uttered by Dr. Manhattan: "Who makes the world?" Snyder thinks that makes perfect sense. "The concept of the super hero has been someone who exacts justice based on their own perspective," he says. "It's when you're trying to decide for the world where the world should be, that you can take that idea all the way and end up inventing a doomsday device that can kill millions of people to create world peace."

Watchmen turned the world of comic books on its head, and Snyder seeks to do the same with super hero films. "In my movie, Superman doesn't care about humanity, Batman can't get it up, and the bad guy wants world peace," he says while laughing, but not kidding. "Will *Watchmen* be the end of super-hero movies? Probably not. But it will sure kick them in the gut." Before *Watchmen*, it was generally assumed that the super heroes, despite some having tortured backgrounds and complicated social lives, at heart possessed motives that were noble and heroic. Now we have to question those motives. Now we have to question just what 'noble' and 'heroic' actually mean. Now we have to

CHAPTER III

"HONOR IS LIKE THE HAWK:
SOMETIMES IT MUST GO HOODED"
– *NEW FRONTIERSMAN, 1985*

THE COMEDIAN

AKA Edward Morgan Blake, played by Jeffrey Dean Morgan

"ME? BITTER? NO.
I THINK IT'S HILARIOUS."

CLASSIFIED

W e know nothing of Edward Blake's formative years, and even less about why he chose the path he did. Barely out of his teens when he burst onto the scene in 1939, Blake had the longest career of any of the costumed crime fighters – that is, before his forced retirement when he plunged to the pavement from his high-rise apartment in October 1985. Giving himself the moniker of the Comedian, the young man in the flamboyant boiler suit made sure his opponents had nothing to laugh at (or frequently with) after he got through with them. Hollis Mason would later describe Blake as "vicious" and "brutal."

However unsavory his methods might have been, Blake quickly made a name for himself cleaning up the New York City waterfront. The Minutemen apparently had no qualms about admitting him as a charter member. Naturally, a group comprised of such intense characters would produce some friction, but Blake went beyond the pale in 1940 when he tried to rape Sally Jupiter (Silk Spectre I) after a Minutemen meeting. Only the timely arrival of Hooded Justice prevented him from completing the act.

CLASSIFIED

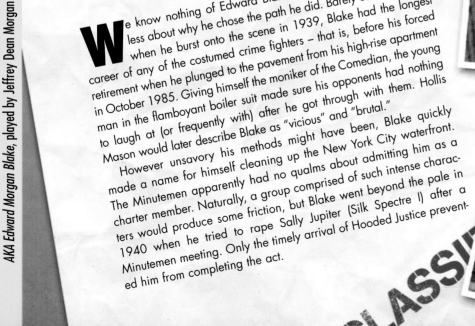

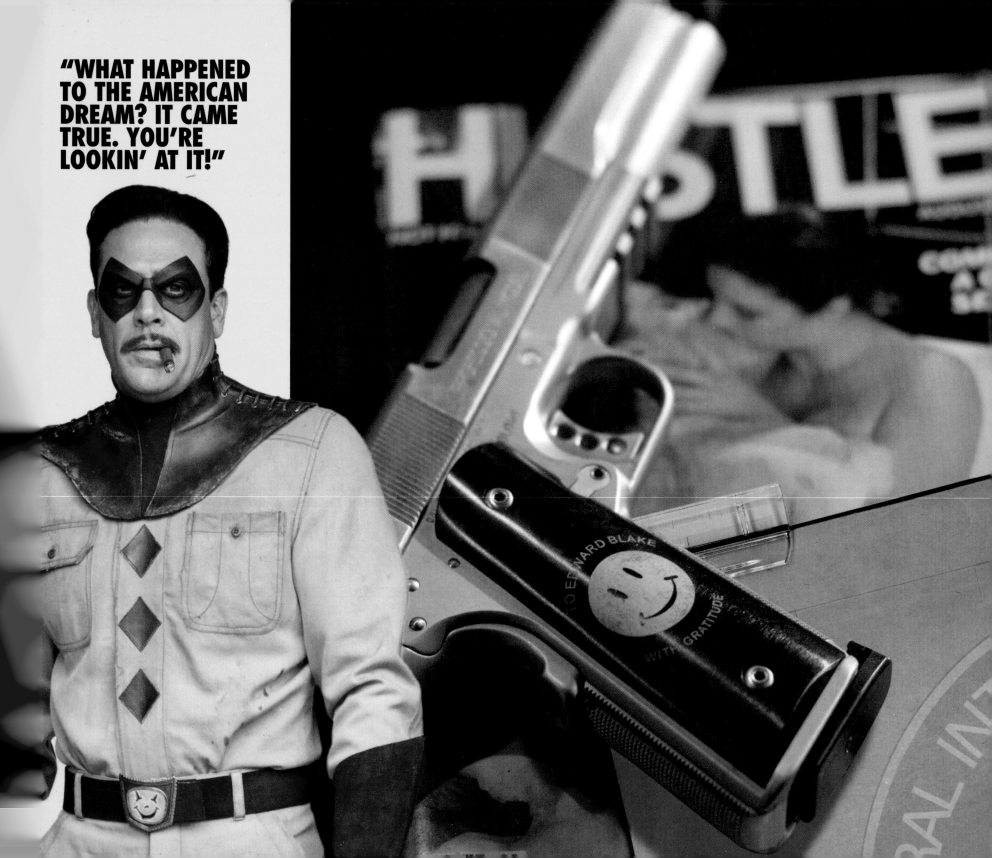

"WHAT HAPPENED TO THE AMERICAN DREAM? IT CAME TRUE. YOU'RE LOOKIN' AT IT!"

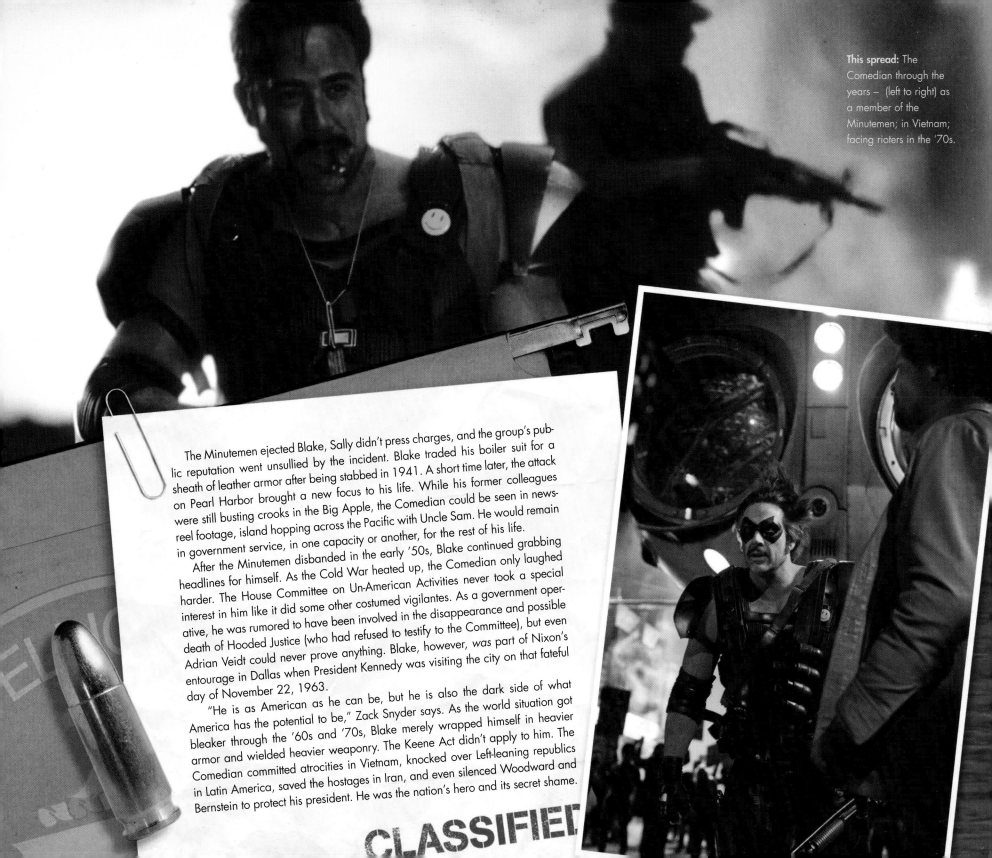

This spread: The Comedian through the years — (left to right) as a member of the Minutemen; in Vietnam; facing rioters in the '70s.

The Minutemen ejected Blake, Sally didn't press charges, and the group's public reputation went unsullied by the incident. Blake traded his boiler suit for a sheath of leather armor after being stabbed in 1941. A short time later, the attack on Pearl Harbor brought a new focus to his life. While his former colleagues were still busting crooks in the Big Apple, the Comedian could be seen in newsreel footage, island hopping across the Pacific with Uncle Sam. He would remain in government service, in one capacity or another, for the rest of his life.

After the Minutemen disbanded in the early '50s, Blake continued grabbing headlines for himself. As the Cold War heated up, the Comedian only laughed harder. The House Committee on Un-American Activities never took a special interest in him like it did some other costumed vigilantes. As a government operative, he was rumored to have been involved in the disappearance and possible death of Hooded Justice (who had refused to testify to the Committee), but even Adrian Veidt could never prove anything. Blake, however, *was* part of Nixon's entourage in Dallas when President Kennedy was visiting the city on that fateful day of November 22, 1963.

"He is as American as he can be, but he is also the dark side of what America has the potential to be," Zack Snyder says. As the world situation got bleaker through the '60s and '70s, Blake merely wrapped himself in heavier armor and wielded heavier weaponry. The Keene Act didn't apply to him. The Comedian committed atrocities in Vietnam, knocked over Left-leaning republics in Latin America, saved the hostages in Iran, and even silenced Woodward and Bernstein to protect his president. He was the nation's hero and its secret shame.

CLASSIFIED

Throughout all his exploits, both immoral and amoral, Blake remained something of an enigma – not least of all to the man cast to play him, Jeffrey Dean Morgan. "Edward Blake is very complicated," says Morgan. "It's been one of the most mentally challenging things I've ever had to do, because the way the Comedian sees the world is much different from the way, say, Jeffrey Dean Morgan does. Every day we find another layer that I didn't think of the day before."

Still, Morgan's job was to find the humanity inside a character who is certainly unlikable, but one you never quite end up hating. "I think he was doing things for the right reason," explains Morgan, "but the things he did in the process, the steps he takes to reach that goal, are horrendous." The face Blake shows to the world is the cynical realist, snickering at the worst the world has to offer and not sweating the small stuff – like body counts.

But Morgan felt there was something beneath the mask: a troubled man who spent his entire life alone. We see that in the very first scene of the film. Sure, he tried at various times to be part of a group – first with the Minutemen, and then with the Watchmen – but he always managed to screw things up. Maybe becoming a vigilante on the streets of New York at such a young age did it, or perhaps it was the horrors of war, but he was never able to form any lasting human bonds. As he tells his archenemy, Moloch, days before his death, "You're the closest thing to a friend I got."

The demands of playing the Comedian – spending much of his time in make-up, getting into his armor, or practicing for a fight – meant that Morgan didn't get to socialize very much with other cast members. He credits this with enhancing the audience's sense of Blake as the lone wolf, as well as heightening the awkward group dynamic when they're all on the screen together. "If I'm not hanging out with these guys 24/7, then it will bring something a little bit different to the set. I don't want to be friendly with anybody in the course of these scenes," Morgan explains, adding, "Obviously, the Comedian's not very friendly to anybody."

"He's a caveman in a lot of ways. He just doesn't have the skill to convey his true feelings," Morgan observes. Nowhere was this fact clearer than during his attempted rape of Sally Jupiter, the one woman he loved in his entire life, but could never be with in a normal relationship. Even after an afternoon's lovemaking in 1953, when he visited Sally and finally let down his guard to give her a peek at the tenderness he was capable of, Blake was unable to maintain the romance over the long haul. The result of that brief liaison was Laurel Jane Juspeczyk, the daughter he never really got to know.

In the end, Blake discovered a plot so terrible, so appalling in scale, even *he* couldn't laugh it off. He appeared almost relieved when death finally came for him. "There's something incredibly sad about the Comedian," says Morgan. "He wants to do good. He wants to have friends. But ultimately, he's just a lost soul."

RORSCHACH

AKA Walter Joseph Kovacs, played by Jackie Earle Haley

"WE DO NOT DO THIS THING BECAUSE IT IS PERMITTED. WE DO IT BECAUSE WE HAVE TO. WE DO IT BECAUSE WE ARE COMPELLED."

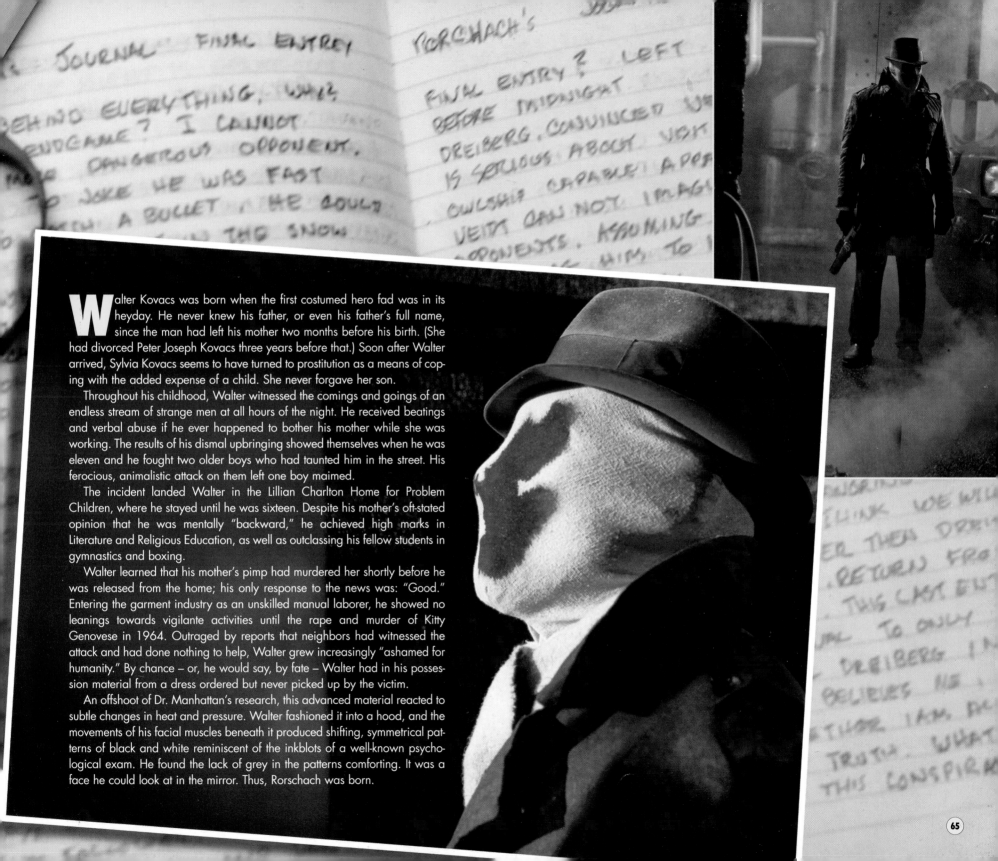

Walter Kovacs was born when the first costumed hero fad was in its heyday. He never knew his father, or even his father's full name, since the man had left his mother two months before his birth. (She had divorced Peter Joseph Kovacs three years before that.) Soon after Walter arrived, Sylvia Kovacs seems to have turned to prostitution as a means of coping with the added expense of a child. She never forgave her son.

Throughout his childhood, Walter witnessed the comings and goings of an endless stream of strange men at all hours of the night. He received beatings and verbal abuse if he ever happened to bother his mother while she was working. The results of his dismal upbringing showed themselves when he was eleven and he fought two older boys who had taunted him in the street. His ferocious, animalistic attack on them left one boy maimed.

The incident landed Walter in the Lillian Charlton Home for Problem Children, where he stayed until he was sixteen. Despite his mother's oft-stated opinion that he was mentally "backward," he achieved high marks in Literature and Religious Education, as well as outclassing his fellow students in gymnastics and boxing.

Walter learned that his mother's pimp had murdered her shortly before he was released from the home; his only response to the news was: "Good." Entering the garment industry as an unskilled manual laborer, he showed no leanings towards vigilante activities until the rape and murder of Kitty Genovese in 1964. Outraged by reports that neighbors had witnessed the attack and had done nothing to help, Walter grew increasingly "ashamed for humanity." By chance – or, he would say, by fate – Walter had in his possession material from a dress ordered but never picked up by the victim.

An offshoot of Dr. Manhattan's research, this advanced material reacted to subtle changes in heat and pressure. Walter fashioned it into a hood, and the movements of his facial muscles beneath it produced shifting, symmetrical patterns of black and white reminiscent of the inkblots of a well-known psychological exam. He found the lack of grey in the patterns comforting. It was a face he could look at in the mirror. Thus, Rorschach was born.

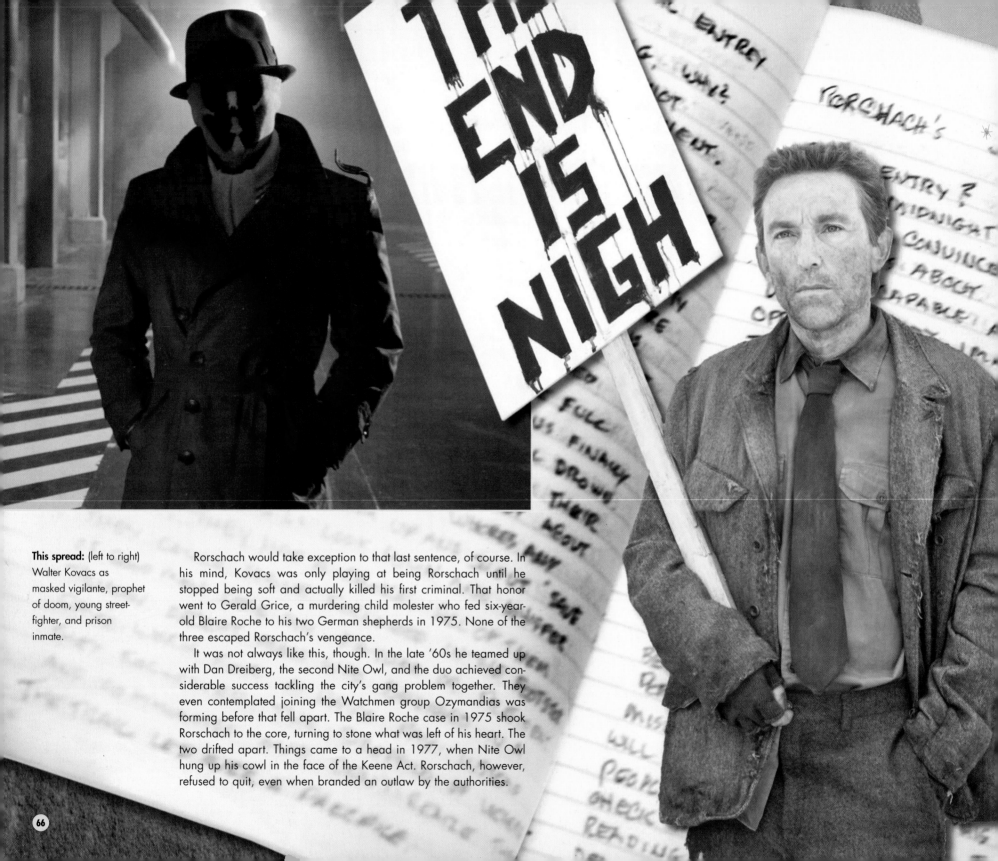

This spread: (left to right) Walter Kovacs as masked vigilante, prophet of doom, young street-fighter, and prison inmate.

Rorschach would take exception to that last sentence, of course. In his mind, Kovacs was only playing at being Rorschach until he stopped being soft and actually killed his first criminal. That honor went to Gerald Grice, a murdering child molester who fed six-year-old Blaire Roche to his two German shepherds in 1975. None of the three escaped Rorschach's vengeance.

It was not always like this, though. In the late '60s he teamed up with Dan Dreiberg, the second Nite Owl, and the duo achieved considerable success tackling the city's gang problem together. They even contemplated joining the Watchmen group Ozymandias was forming before that fell apart. The Blaire Roche case in 1975 shook Rorschach to the core, turning to stone what was left of his heart. The two drifted apart. Things came to a head in 1977, when Nite Owl hung up his cowl in the face of the Keene Act. Rorschach, however, refused to quit, even when branded an outlaw by the authorities.

Quitting was never an option for Rorschach, because becoming a masked avenger was never a choice, but a calling. "Little Walter Kovacs just didn't stand much of a chance, you know? He's one messed up individual," says the man behind the inkblot mask, Jackie Earle Haley. "I think every bit of vigilante work he does is protecting that inner child. With every cleaver strike and every finger break, he's protecting the child that he was. He's striking out and smacking his mom."

Perhaps because of his past, the one thing Rorschach never loses sight of is the victim. Someone has been wronged, and that needs to be redressed. Period. "We really do live in a complex world, a world of shades of grey. And Walter has just been such a victim of that," Haley points out. "For him, that complexity, that bullshit grey, simply justifies the continued victimization of himself and everybody who suffers from someone else's special interest. He had to make the world a place of black and white."

"HUMANS ARE SAVAGE IN NATURE. NO MATTER HOW MUCH YOU TRY TO DRESS IT UP, TO DISGUISE IT."

Above: Trying to evade arrest at Moloch's apartment.

Opposite: Rorschach on the streets of New York, and sneaking into Dr. Manhattan's lab.

Rorschach views everything through this extreme filter of light and dark, passing judgment with moral certitude on everyone and everything he comes into contact with. Sometimes he feels the need to act on those judgments, but more often he simply jots them down in a weathered notebook. His voiced journal entries give us a unique insight into Rorschach's mind that we don't get with other characters. "Rorschach is this uncompromising, unrelenting seeker of justice in a noirish, throwback style," says director Zack Snyder. "He's also the narrator of the film. He's constantly commenting on society, on the other characters, and on the mystery that's unfolding. He's the one that drives us through that mystery."

But why? Why is he fixated on solving the murder of Edward Blake when the world is teetering on the edge of nuclear war? The answer could be that, like Blake, Rorschach craves the camaraderie he can never have. "There's nobody in this guy's life. The

only people that he really does have are the other masks," Haley explains. "And when he stumbles upon this murder of this mask, he's going to investigate it. He's going to find out what the hell's going on." It also gives him an excuse to seek out old acquaintances, and perhaps rekindle relationships with these once-like-minded people.

Abused child? Avenger of the weak? Obsessed moral crusader? Lonely, middle-aged man? Rorschach is all these things and perhaps one more. "If I had to put down one thing for Rorschach, it's that he's after the truth. That's all he cares about, regardless of how he gets there and who gets hurt," muses editor William Hoy. Certainly at Karnak, his unyielding resolve to cling to the truth, no matter what the consequences for himself or the world, is ultimately what dooms him. Given the choice between living with a lie and suffering obliteration, he readily chooses the latter.

NITE OWL II

AKA Daniel Dreiberg, played by Patrick Wilson

Dan Dreiberg had always dreamed of flying. As a child, his mind raced with flights of fantasy inspired by tales from classical mythology, the Arabian Nights, and medieval romances of questing knights. When he grew a bit older, Dan delved into the practical study of birds and airplanes, eventually graduating with dual Master's degrees in Zoology and Aeronautics from Harvard. His father, a banker, had always been irked that Dan had showed no interest in the same career path; nevertheless, he left his son a considerable fortune when he passed away. "Rich" and "bored" was how Dan described himself at that time in his life.

Through it all, he never lost his boyhood fascination with magical adventure stories where the good always emerged triumphant. "I think he always had this romantic fantasy of being a super hero and saving the girl," says Patrick Wilson, who embodies the role of Dan. An interesting fact that says a lot about Dan's character is that, unlike all the other costumed vigilantes, he's the only one that felt the need to ask permission to take up the hero's mantle. He actually wrote to his long-time

idol, Hollis Mason, soon after the elder Nite Owl retired, requesting to carry on the name. The fact that others were still dressing up to fight crime also legitimized the career choice in his mind.

With his engineering background and sizeable monetary resources, Dan created an impressive array of hardware that took the Nite Owl brand to new heights – literally. Aside from developing several different high-tech suits for working in various environments, night-vision goggles, and pocket lasers, Dan had to have been most proud of his flying, submersible Owlship, which he dubbed "Archie" after Archimedes, Merlin's owl in T. H. White's *The Once and Future King*.

Designed to be stealthy – whether cruising undetected beneath the East River or hovering overhead with fogscreens on full, its round shape evading even military radar – Archie also sported heavy weaponry such as sonic screechers, a flamethrower, a Gatling gun, and air-to-air missiles. "The design of the ship is very faithful to the comic. I mean, when I walked in it for the first time, I was blown away. It's unbelievable detail in there. I could sit in there – and I have – for hours," admits Wilson.

"I'M JUST TIRED OF BEING AFRAID. AFRAID OF WAR, AFRAID OF THE MASK KILLER, AFRAID OF THIS DAMN COSTUME AND HOW MUCH I NEED IT."

This spread: Nite Owl II and Dan Dreiberg – two very different sides of the same man.

"THERE WERE ENOUGH OTHER GUYS DOING IT SO I DIDN'T FEEL RIDICULOUS... I FELT SO CONNECTED. YOU KNOW? TO SOMETHING THAT MATTERED."

Dan also designed and built a gas-powered grappling gun fo Rorschach, his crime-busting partner for over a decade. Thei fighting styles complemented each other perfectly: Rorschach the cagey scrapper, punctuated by moments of explosive volatility, while Nite Owl relied on gadgetry and his power ful fists to take down the bad guys. Together they smashed Big Figure's mob, and were making other inroads into New York's gang problem when, in 1970, Nite Owl sug gested they try joining forces with a group called the Watchmen that was just forming. When that effort fe apart, Dan saw his lifelong dream of being part of c brotherhood of heroes dying with it. The Keene Ac put the final nail in that coffin.

Hollis Mason and Dan continued to maintair a close connection over the years, with Hollis fil ing the roles of mentor and surrogate father That bond was especially important to Dar after his early retirement in '77, which wa also when his relationship with the increasing ly brutal Rorschach went on hiatus. His weekl visits to drink beer at Hollis' place were hal reminiscences about the glory days and hal therapy sessions. "Once Dan retired, he want ed to know how to cope with being out of the limelight. 'What happens when you take off that suit? How do you deal with it?' That's what he seeks in Hollis," observes Wilson.

At the beginning of the film, "Dan's a broken guy. When the Watchmen were retired, he never moved on with himself," points out Zack Snyder. "When he was Nite Owl he was complete, and he doesn't really know that. Now he feels something's missing from his life and doesn't know what it is."

Dan's sense of loss and lack of direction come across partly in the way he's let himself go over the years. Snyder saw the weight gain as a visual metaphor for what has been going on in the man's life, although he didn't want a fat Dan by any means. "When you meet Dan, he's been out of it for a few years. So, I ended up gaining about twenty-five pounds," says Wilson. "Nobody ever asked me to, but I felt with that much weight I could feel a little bigger, and maybe wear the pants a bit dumpier. Show how he's gotten soft – physically, politically, sexually."

Then Rorschach shows up, talking crazy about being on the trail of a mask killer. Dan dismisses the idea, but the visit rattles him. He begins to examine how he has just been marking time all these years, while Rorschach has been on the streets and keeping the faith. "No matter how twisted the guy's views are, he's still fighting the fight, and I think Dan really envies that in a weird way," explains Wilson.

Right: Nite Owl II suited up for Antarctica.

Opposite top: Dan loses his cool.

Opposite bottom: Dan is about to lose his mojo, as seen through his own goggles.

But what ultimately pulls Dan out of his slump isn't his reconnection with Rorschach, and it isn't the threat of some shadowy mask killer. It's getting up the courage to put his costume back on. "His struggle throughout is that the costume is him at his best. It's what he strives to be," Wilson says. "Until he has that on, he's completely emasculated. He just doesn't have an identity. I would imagine it's very much like a soldier that goes to war and comes back home and doesn't know whether he can fit in."

Getting back in costume is not as easy as it sounds. "The crux of Dan is he is terrified to put the suit on, but he cannot really live without being Nite Owl," explains Wilson. Part of that terror comes from his worldview. Dan has an old-fashioned sense of law and order, and the authorities have outlawed costumed vigilantes; in dressing up, he would essentially have to become what he's sworn to fight. Another part of his reticence comes from an intimate knowledge of the mental toll donning a mask has taken on others, especially Rorschach. Lastly, putting it on would be admitting he needs it.

Enter Laurie Juspeczyk. She's outspoken, outgoing, rebellious – everything Dan isn't. There's an attraction there certainly, but more importantly they bond over tales of their crime-fighting pasts. They never actually worked together back in the day, but Dan soon finds in Laurie someone who's experienced what he has, someone he can relate to, and someone he can kick major butt with.

Although their first fumbling attempt at lovemaking ends with Dan unable to perform, it's Laurie who suggests taking Archie out to clear their minds. After suiting up and rescuing folks from a tenement fire, she discovers a whole new Dan. "She's the one who opens me up to putting the suit on again," says Wilson. "I think I just needed somebody to look me in the eye and say, 'Let's do it. I'll do it with you.'" He essentially needed permission to be himself – but that's just how Dan is.

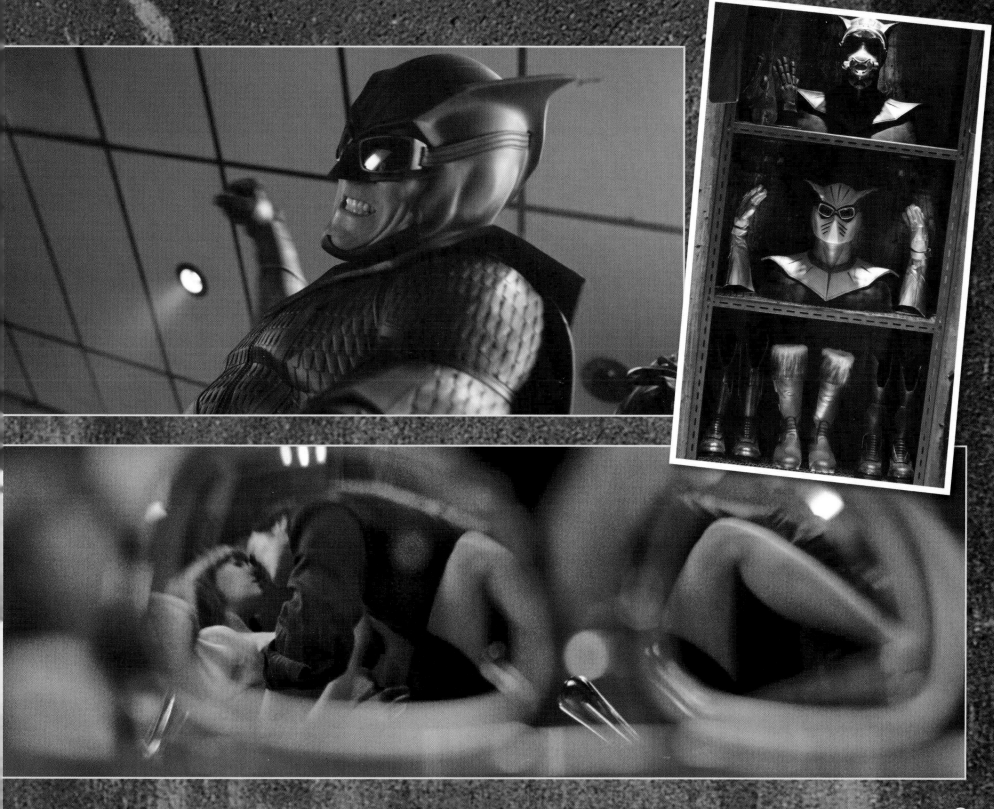

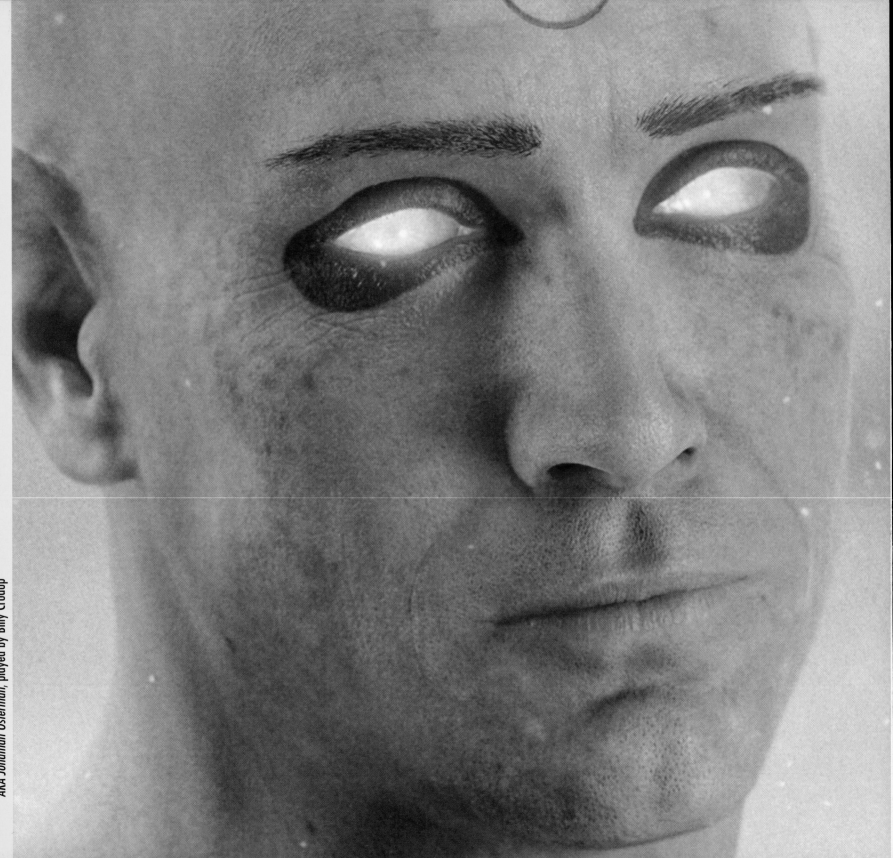

DR. MANHATTAN

AKA Jonathan Osterman, played by Billy Crudup

A native of Brooklyn, New York, Jon Osterman had planned to follow his father into watch repair. After learning of the bombing of Hiroshima and Einstein's declaration that time was merely a relative concept, Jon's father insisted he instead study the profession of the future – atomic physics. Ever the dutiful son, Jon graduated with a Ph.D. from Princeton in 1958 and soon after started work at the Gila Flats Test Base in Arizona. There he met fellow scientist Wally Weaver, as well as the outgoing Janey Slater, who would quickly become his girlfriend.

In August, 1959, Jon entered the Intrinsic Field Separation Chamber to retrieve his watch, only to be sealed in when the automatic time lock initiated. As the air inside the chamber warmed and became charged with static electricity, Jon grasped the horrifying fate that awaited him. Janey couldn't watch. The particle cannons fired, ripping him to pieces at the subatomic level. The human being known as Jon Osterman ceased to exist.

Clockwise from below: Dr. Manhattan prepares to disassemble a tank; a simple hydrogen atom will do as a personal symbol; gangsters scatter before him; Jon gets blindsided by audience questions during his Ted Koppel interview.

Later that autumn, workers at Gila Flats witnessed Jon's grisly attempts to piece himself back together – a circulatory system here, a partially muscled skeleton there – culminating in his astonishing reappearance in the base lunch room in a burst of ultraviolet light. After assessing his superhuman abilities to manipulate matter, the Pentagon drafted Jon into government service as the mainstay of the American strategic deterrent. They dubbed him Dr. Manhattan, "for the ominous associations it will raise in America's enemies." Jon observed that they were shaping him "into something gaudy and lethal," but he allowed it to happen without protest.

"He is kind of an archetypical '50s male," explains actor Billy Crudup. "He believes in the goodness of his country, believes in the virtues of following the designs of your leaders." At the government's urging, the superhuman being even took up the mantle of crime fighting, with gruesome results. "If Superman grabbed your arm and pulled really hard, he'd pull your arm out of the socket. That's the thing you don't see in a Superman movie," says director Zack Snyder, calling into question exactly what it means to be heroic – a repeated theme of *Watchmen*.

"THEY CALL ME DR. MANHATTAN. THEY EXPLAIN THE NAME HAS BEEN CHOSEN FOR THE OMINOUS ASSOCIATIONS IT WILL RAISE IN AMERICA'S ENEMIES. THEY ARE SHAPING ME INTO SOMETHING GAUDY... SOMETHING LETHAL."

78

But Crudup is quick to point out that Dr. Manhattan is nothing like the costumed heroes that preceded him. "They were people who played dress up. They were vigilantes, and they don't believe in the community's capacity to take care of itself," he says. "Osterman is the exact opposite. He is someone who is by the book, believes in the stability of his country and the morality of his government, and would do whatever they wanted. And consequently, as Dr. Manhattan, he does just that."

Dr. Manhattan's unquestioning patriotism was demonstrated most dramatically in 1971, when he agreed to President Nixon's request that he intervene in Vietnam. His appearance on the battlefield ended the conflict in a matter of days. Many of his enemies surrendered to him with "an almost religious awe." During the victory celebrations that followed, he watched Edward Blake – the Comedian – murder the mother of Blake's own unborn child, but was unmoved to stop it. Even as his need to wear clothing dissipated, Dr. Manhattan's link to humanity was diminishing. Janey Slater sensed it and left the unaging man-god years ago while he was starting to take up with a very young Laurie Juspeczyk.

"I DON'T THINK THERE IS A GOD... AND IF THERE IS, I AM NOTHING LIKE HIM."

"I AM TIRED OF EARTH, THESE PEOPLE. I AM TIRED OF BEING CAUGHT IN THE TANGLE OF THEIR LIVES."

This spread: Having left Earth, Dr. Manhattan contemplates his past.

One of the factors that drove a wedge between Dr. Manhattan and the rest of the human race was the fact that he does not experience time in the way everyone else does. While not omniscient, he can look into his own past, present, and future simultaneously. The fact that he can see things before they happen, however, doesn't always mean he can change them. Time seems relatively immutable. As he tells Laurie on Mars, "We're all puppets, Laurie. I'm just a puppet who can see the strings."

Crudup found playing such a prescient character placed unusual demands on his skills as an actor. "Most of the tools I deal with are about motivation and about objectives, and what people do when they want things," he explains. "So, to play someone who doesn't worry about expectations because he knows his entire future really throws a wrench into the conventional tools for playing a scene. I don't think I expected it to be as difficult, day to day, as it really was."

In particular, Dr. Manhattan's conversations with Laurie tested Crudup's abilities to their greatest extent. "Exactly the thing I found most difficult and frustrating is when I say things like, 'In this conversation, you're going to reveal something to me and I'm going to be surprised by it.' That's a really hard thing to play, because he's not pretending when he's surprised." Crudup found he needed to set up and maintain parallel yet separate narratives in his head: one where Dr. Manhattan interacts as if he doesn't know the future, and another, where he is an observer commenting on that interaction before it happens.

JUNE · 1959

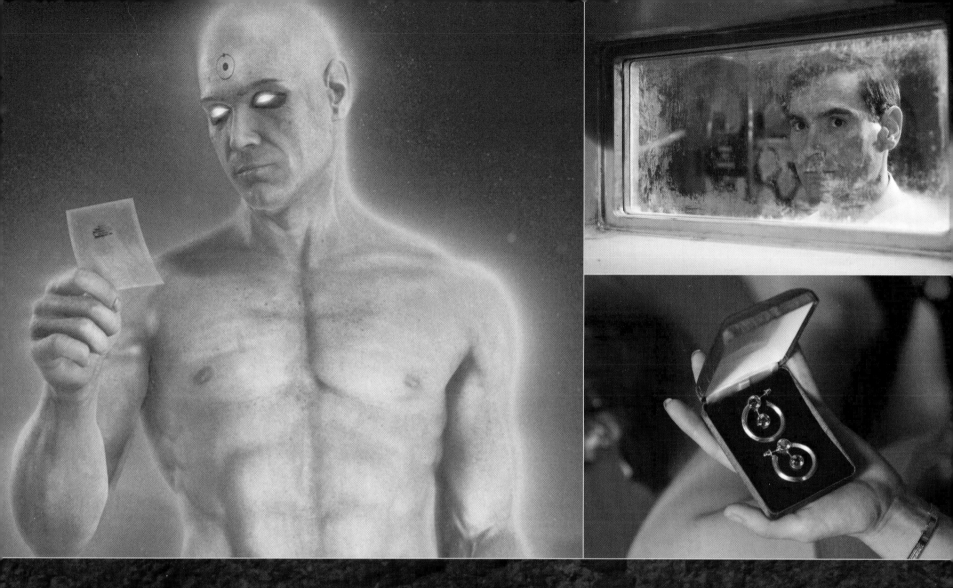

One of Jon Osterman's central character traits – his intense interest in the inner workings of the universe – also tended to tug him further and further from humanity the longer he spent as Dr. Manhattan. "Physics is an ordered world to be discovered, and human interaction is a chaotic world to be taught through harsh experience," explains Crudup, "and so I think once he's given the opportunity to observe the physical world in such an incredible way, he becomes completely disillusioned with human experience. He goes from antipathy to apathy. He has a vision of the world that no longer includes humans."

This is one of the major conundrums posed by the graphic novel and the film. As Snyder puts it: "If you have a super being that can do anything, and he's like a god, what happens when he starts to get annoyed with these human creatures that he's pledged to defend? What happens when he decides that's not a thing worth his time?"

During the events of *Watchmen*, a burst of tachyons prevents him from seeing the immediate future clearly, and for the first time it becomes truly possible to surprise Dr. Manhattan. Tricked into believing he has given cancer to several of his closest past associates, coupled with Laurie leaving him, he loses his final link to the world and leaves the Earth for a self-imposed exile on Mars. As the story unfolds, it remains to be seen if the world's only superman can prevent Armageddon – or if he even cares to.

"WHY'D WE DO IT, DAN? DRESS UP LIKE THAT... I THINK THE KEENE ACT WAS THE BEST THING THAT EVER HAPPENED TO US."

SILK SPECTRE

AKA Laurel Jane Juspeczyk, played by Malin Akerman

Laurie's birth in 1953 spelled the end of her mother's crime-fighting career. Many of her earliest memories were of her parents bickering. Some of it was about money and some of it was about work, but underlying it all was an issue Laurie wouldn't understand until much later – the identity of her real father. As strange as it seems, Sally had had an afternoon tryst with the Comedian in the early '50s, producing Laurie. The quarrels only got worse with time. When her parents' marriage ended in divorce, Laurie sought to put some figurative distance between her parents and herself, choosing to go by her mother's birth name.

Not that anyone could ever mistake Laurie for anything other than Sally Jupiter's daughter – and the similarities go beyond good looks. "Laurie is this regular girl who got born into a crazy situation. From a very young age, she has been in training to become a super hero just like her mother was," explains Malin Akerman. Her molding included daily workouts alone in the home gym, schooling in various styles of fighting, and being fitted with a tight and sexy costume to beguile the criminals, just like Sally did.

Laurie was ambivalent about the whole concept of being a crime fighter, but she did what was expected of her. Akerman says, "It's sort of like being trained as an athlete from a very young age, but the difference is that it's not a coach, it's your mother. There aren't many other choices. Laurie has been put into a life that wasn't necessarily chosen by her." It can certainly be argued that this pressure to reprise her mother's successful crime-fighting career drove an even wider wedge between Laurie and Sally.

At the age of seventeen, Laurie made her debut in the world of costumed adventurers at the first (and last) meeting of the Watchmen. Although the Comedian impressed her the most with his no-bullshit attitude, she found herself exchanging furtive glances with the one veritable super hero in the group, Dr. Manhattan – a fact that didn't go unnoticed by Jon's then-girlfriend, Janey Slater.

Dating a walking strategic deterrent, however physically perfect he appeared, might have been too intimidating for most girls, but not Laurie. It also might have helped that her mother was put off by his strangeness. Billy Crudup explains, "She got involved with him when she was very young, and there was probably something kind of exotic about it. But it's the sort of thing that you do, as you become a young adult, and you begin to realize the ways in which your parents have shaped you."

Akerman sees their early relationship as something impetuous and bordering on fantasy fulfillment. "Dr. Manhattan is like this guy that you've seen from afar, this untouchable guy that you never could have

"I USED TO BE A MASKED AVENGER TOO... I'M USED TO GOING OUT AT THREE IN THE MORNING AND DOING SOMETHING STUPID."

in high school, and you get him and it's just so crazy and insane. The emotions are out of control," she says. Getting together with Jon also got Laurie out of her parents' house. And the ageless Dr. Manhattan (who either still had human wants and desires at this point, or was pretending to) got a young, pretty lover in exchange for the old.

Apart from playing opposite a cold, logical super-being, Akerman found that the time lapse in the film made it difficult to portray an evolved relationship, which they as characters never went through. She says she needed to dig into personal experiences to piece the performance together. "We pretty much jump right to the end of our relationship," Akerman explains. "The biggest challenge was trying to figure out how his addiction to his craft and him becoming less and less of a person would affect me. I've had one bad relationship where somebody chose something other than me, and that resonated really deeply. You can feel when someone falls out of love with you."

The same was not true of Laurie's relationship with Dan Dreiberg (Nite Owl II), as they spent plenty of time onscreen getting to know each other. "Patrick (Wilson) and I actually got a chance to have scenes together," says Akerman. "What you guys see us go through is us having real moments with each other, and our relationship is growing at more of a regular pace." A big part of that relationship – developing through several harrowing, adrenaline-charged incidents – is the mutual discovery that being costumed adventurers is what they were meant to be all along. As Akerman puts it, "They give each other another reason to live again."

"Laurie resents her mother for pushing her into this line of work," says Zack Snyder, "but only through the course of the film does she realize that it wasn't her mother, it was her. Once she gets her costume on like the old days, and she's standing there in a burning building, you realize this is her gift." Editor William Hoy sees the parallels in parenting. "It's like you push your daughter to take piano lessons. They're pretty good at it, but they hate it. At some point they figure out they can actually play keyboards in a rock and roll band, and it's like, 'Hey, I'm actually having fun here,'" he says.

It's that discovery about her own self that leads Laurie to find a new respect for her mother. "Laurie saw the silliness in her mother more than the aspects that were actually kind of amazing about what she instigated and what she created," explains Carla Gugino, who played Sally. "And Laurie's journey then comes back around to understanding that in the end of the story."

While Laurie was Dr. Manhattan's tenuous link to humanity, her bond with Dan becomes her real link back to it. "Reconnecting with Dan gives me an identity as a woman – someone actually looking at me, one human being to another, for the first time in I don't know how many years," Akerman explains. Without that bond, she might have driven down the same path as her mother, a depressing little road paved with bottles and memories.

Having the right man and the right career simultaneously represents a break in the cycle of lost dreams of past generations. "Laurie has a beautiful arc in this film," says Akerman. "She gets to get out of the rut. Sally never got the happy ending with Hollis, whereas Dan and Laurie actually get the happy ending." After all the turmoil, pain, and death they have endured, that's a nice sliver of hope to hold on to.

This spread: (left to right) Laurie and Dan, Silk Spectre II and Nite Owl II – a new partnership in

"IT'S EASIER TO BLAME IT ALL ON MY MOM. BUT THE TRUTH? I COULD'VE SAID NO."

OZYMANDIAS

AKA Adrian Veidt, played by Matthew Goode

"I RESOLVED TO APPLY ANTIQUITY'S TEACHINGS TO OUR WORLD, TODAY. SO BEGAN *MY* PATH TO CONQUEST – CONQUEST NOT OF MEN, BUT OF THE EVILS THAT BESET THEM."

Despite being one of the few masked heroes to reveal his identity to the world, Adrian Veidt remains of the great mysteries of *Watchmen*. His alter ego, Ozymandias (the Greek name for the Egyptian pharaoh Rameses II), burst onto the scene and began smashing drug smuggling operations at about the same time Jon Osterman was experiencing his nuclear accident. He was one of what Hollis Mason called the 'New Breed' of costumed adventurers. Between the failure to bring the Watchmen together in 1970 and the Keene Act in 1977, he dropped his mask and formed the many-armed conglomerate Veidt Enterprises, earning billions with his supra-genius-level intellect. In 1985, he perpetrated a vast hoax that claimed fifteen million lives in an effort to secure world peace.

These, of course, are merely the bare facts of his career. The graphic novel only provides us with just a few more tantalizing bits of his backstory. The son of wealthy immigrants Ingrid Renata and Friedrich Werner Veidt, Adrian learned to hide his extraordinary intelligence at a young age because of the suspicion it aroused in others. At seventeen, with his parents dead, he gave away his inheritance to show what he could achieve on his own – just like the man he admired most from all of human history, Alexander the Great. Adrian retraced the path of Alexander's victorious army through the Near and Middle East; he continued deep into Asia, where he learned martial arts. On his return, he necessarily had to stop in Alexandria, Egypt. There he took hashish and had earth-shattering visions in the desert that convinced him that the wisdom of the pharaohs lived on through him.

At least, that's how Adrian told it to his devoted scientists at his Antarctic retreat of Karnak before he poisoned them. Deciding how much of that was real, and how much more needed to be filled in, is part of the job of the actor. Matthew Goode, the last-minute choice to portray Adrian Veidt, says, "His whole thing is about hiding, and what's real and what isn't. No one has any grasp of what's going on in that man's head at any given time. It's all a façade. He's the unknowable." Obviously, this was a crucial trait to possess in order to carry out his shocking master plan successfully. Certainly no one, including his closest friends in the costumed adventurer community, ever guessed what he was capable of.

Opposite: Ozymandias – ready to save the world.

Below left: Veidt pays a visit to the Comedian.
Right top: The captains of industry get an earful.
Right bottom: Mission accomplished.

In exploring the idea of why Adrian would give his wealth away and set himself up as a savior for all humanity, Goode felt family guilt might have played a huge part. "I thought it was more interesting and in line with the sort of myths that you get in comics, and more operatic, if his parents had been Nazis," explains Goode.

If his family's money came from profiting from the Third Reich's war, or was even stolen directly from murdered Jews, it made sense that Adrian would want to reinvent himself and make amends. "It goes with his moral story, and it also fits very nicely with the idea of the American Dream. Coming from that, it makes him more likable to play as well," says Goode.

While the inclusion of such a background didn't change the story at all, it injected certain nuances into Goode's performance that meshed well with the idea that Adrian is not all that he seems. "His public persona is incredibly American. He has the accent, too, so everybody thinks they know Adrian," Goode points out. There is a subtle change in his voice, however, when he is speaking in private, particularly with old comrades-in-arms like Dan Dreiberg. "It's a mix of German and American, and that's who he really is," says Goode.

This spread: Veidt manipulates an aggressive reporter (opposite top) and a hired assassin (opposite bottom) to help him carry out his master plan.

One could even make the case that appearances are a bit of an obsession with Adrian. Apart from owning a company that manufactures cosmetics, hair-care products, and high-fashion sportswear, he's always dressed in the latest style and can often be seen out at the trendiest nightspots.

Another of his defining characteristics is his superb physique and tip-top conditioning, as the Comedian found out. Although just as old as the other masks of his generation, "as opposed to the others who've aged slightly, because of this supreme fitness regimen he sticks to, he looks very like he did back in the day. He's this incredible physical specimen," says Goode. "God knows what I'm doing playing the part," he adds with a laugh.

Goode is also quick to point out that Adrian's vanity could have been just an act, given that his motives were really quite noble. "He looks like he's an arrogant son of a bitch with a huge ego, selling his image to

"IT DOESN'T TAKE A GENIUS TO SEE THAT THE WORLD HAS PROBLEMS."

make millions and billions of dollars. The conceit is that he loves the lifestyle and he loves the money," says Goode, "but he's the most self-less character of them all, really, because there's no real benefits for him. And even though he's going to end up saving the world, it's set up so that he doesn't take any credit for it in the slightest."

His ultimate motives really stem back to the abortive meeting of the Watchmen, when his eyes were opened to the fact that bumping heads with criminals would never solve the real ills of the world. Goode explains, "He realizes due to a conversation with the Comedian – which he probably loathed at the time, the fact that the Comedian was right – that the scale they were working on just wasn't up to scratch." This led him to give up crime fighting to concentrate on marketing products in order to fund his research – both for humanity's immediate gain, and for the sake of his master plan to convince the world that a bigger enemy is out there.

The morality of Adrian's choice, which he took upon himself to make for the rest of the world, goes to the core of what *Watchmen* is about. It produces more questions than it does answers. "He does something horrific to save billions, and is that right or wrong?" asks Zack Snyder. "You know, these are the things that super heroes would be doing eventually, if you give them enough time... Or it's fun to imagine they would."

Editor William Hoy, however, sees Adrian's slaughter of millions as simply the culmination of the many bad things that can emerge from an inflated ego. He says, "He's doing what he thinks is right. All these mad-men in our history, they obviously were doing what they thought was right, too." Perhaps in the end, Adrian learned the wrong lessons from the past. After all, it was Hitler who said, "The bigger the lie, the more the people will believe it."

After stints as a waitress and a burlesque dancer, Sally Jupiter became the first female costumed vigilante in 1939. Some say it was her agent, Laurence Schexnayder, who pushed her into joining the burgeoning hero fad, but make no mistake about it, Sally enjoyed the life – especially the publicity. "Sally definitely wanted to fight crime. She was out there actually putting herself in danger, getting the bad guys, using her feminine wiles," says Carla Gugino, "but she also wanted the attention and to be in the limelight – and she wanted to use her looks in order to do that."

When first contacted by Captain Metropolis about the possibility of combining their efforts in the war on crime, Sally thought the whole thing was a gag. Schexnayder, however, convinced her that such an association could be a public relations coup, and it was he who took out the large ad in the *New York Gazette* to attract more costumed heroes to the cause. They called themselves the 'Minutemen' (although two of the eight were women), and their exploits captured the nation's imagination at a time when the Axis Powers were fanning the flames of war.

"THINGS ARE TOUGH ALL OVER, CUPCAKE. IT RAINS ON THE JUST AND UNJUST ALIKE."

Above and left: Sally Jupiter's fateful encounter with the Comedian in 1940.

But life was far from perfect in their little private world of costumed heroes. Most significantly, the Comedian attempted to rape Sally one night after a meeting in 1940. Such were the mores of the time that she harbored some guilt about it, as though her provocative dress and manner had invited the attack. "When the Minutemen came together, there was a great sense of innocence," explains Gugino. "And even though her sexuality was always right out there, I think it came from a place that was really much more naïve. This thing that happens with the Comedian, this huge event that shapes the rest of her life, really was a wake-up call in a very brutal way."

Through the rest of the '40s, Sally tried to put the incident behind her as she garnered her fair share of headlines – or perhaps more than her share, given her photogenic appearance. She skillfully used the exposure to best advantage as a springboard into a successful modeling career. "She felt like she had to go out and get her own. She wasn't going to be a housewife – that was not in her DNA," says Gugino. All the top artists and photographers of the day clamored to capture her image, and she became one of the GIs' favorite wartime pinup girls. Any American alive during that period would be able to describe the nose art on that most famous B-29 bomber, Miss Jupiter, which dropped its atomic payload on Hiroshima.

Some have compared Sally to other sexy and extroverted women, such as Annie Oakley, Bettie Page, and Mae West. "Sally may be more like Mae West – I mean, she's got these great one-liners like that – but she might think of herself a little more like Rita Hayworth in Gilda," Gugino points out. "That's the great juxtaposition with her, that she would like to think of herself as just possibly a little more polished than she really is." Certainly she never reached the stardom of either West or Hayworth, starring in only a single film, Silk Swingers of Suburbia, which was deemed by at least one critic as "too awful even to be dignified with the term 'pornography.'"

Scandals, insanity, and deaths in the line of duty plagued the Minutemen heading into the '50s, but Sally's pregnancy and retirement were what really did the group in. She had been the glue that had held it together, and with her gone the remaining members felt more and more like silly, aging men in tights. Sally had married her agent years before, and he exited the group with her, leaving the Minutemen without a publicity department. The masked fraternity folded soon after.

Modeling jobs **began** to dry up with her fading looks, and Sally found herself looking **down** the barrel of a long retirement trapped in an increasingly rocky and loveless marriage. Schexnayder couldn't stomach the fact that Sally had allowed the Comedian into her bed after what he had done to her years before; coupled with the constant reminder that Laurie was not his, it all became more than he could take. After spending more than a decade shouting at one another, he and Sally divorced in the late '60s. Sally pushed her cocktail hour earlier and earlier, and it grew **longer** and longer.

The one bright spot in her life while everything else was getting dimmer was, of course, **Laurie**. Sally pushed little Laurel Jane into becoming a costumed vigilante from an early age, perhaps believing the girl could obtain heights she never did, but it all came at a price. "There's a lot of the element of living through her daughter, which is a classic mother/daughter dynamic. She has been an overbearing mother and she's projected a lot on her child. There's a lot of tension in their relationship," says Gugino. "In truth, that comes out of insecurity, and at the end of the day, she'd give her life for her in a second. There is no doubt that there's no one that **Sally** loves more than her daughter."

That includes Edward Blake, who couldn't lower his guard for very long, or Hollis Mason, who waited too long to pick up the phone and call her. So, Sally lives out her golden years in a nostalgic sort of loneliness, but happy to **have** reconciled with Laurie at least. In many ways, Sally's life is like a **microcosm** of the world of *Watchmen* – a bittersweet study in what might **have** been.

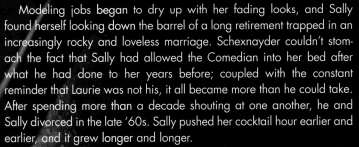

Opposite: A retired super hero in Palm Springs.

Right: Young Laurie's view of her mother's marriage coming to an end.

NITE OWL

AKA Hollis Mason, played by Stephen McHattie & Clint Carleton

"IT STARTED WITH THE GANGS... NOBODY COULD PICK 'EM OUT OF A LINEUP 'CAUSE OF THE DAMN MASKS. SO, A FEW OF US COPS DECIDED TO MASK UP, TOO – FINISH WHAT THE LAW COULDN'T."

Hollis Mason moved to New York City with his family from their Montana farmstead when he was twelve. His eponymous grandfather opposed the move on the grounds that the big city would corrupt the moral fiber of anyone who stepped foot in it. He needn't have worried about his grandson, though. Too much country decency remained in the boy for Gotham to have any deleterious effect. Hollis helped his father out at Moe Vernon's garage, got decent grades, and went on to graduate from the NYPD Police Academy in 1938.

Hollis had always been fond of the adventure pulps growing up – the Shadow, Doc Savage, that sort of thing. In his adolescence he had often fantasized about saving girls from malevolent forces; sometimes they were classmates, sometimes a favorite teacher. When he was a young patrolman walking his first beats, he noticed the kids reading comic books with new heroes in them – super heroes, in fact.

They struck a chord with Hollis. They embodied an unambiguous morality that even his beloved pulps lacked, and he devoured them (surreptitiously, lest his maturity be questioned) whenever he could. His mind only began to swirl with the possibilities open to him, however, when the costumed heroes leapt off the comic panels and onto the newspaper headlines. Hooded Justice was the first; Hollis vowed to be the second.

BY
HOLLIS
MASON
A.K.A. NITE OWL

UNDER THE HOOD

AN AUTOBIOGRAPHY

UNDER THE HOOD

He spent three months training night and day at the police gymnasium, a schedule that usually saw him in bed by nine, and thus left little time for after-hours socializing with his fellow cops. One of them took to sarcastically calling him 'Night Owl.' Hollis adopted it as his persona, and designed a costume to match. What was essentially a short-sleeved leather leotard with a hood gave him core protection (with an extra reinforcing of chain mail on the briefs and head), leaving his legs and arms free for action. He eschewed the use of a cape because it was "too unwieldy." He later secured his mask with spirit gum after his first one got pulled down over his eyes in a fight with a drunk, thus demonstrating to him the vulnerabilities of string.

He began patrolling the streets of his neighborhood in early '39, and was soon followed by a bevy of others itching to get in on the fad. By fall of that year he and seven others had joined forces as the charter members of the Minutemen. They had some spectacular early successes taking down crooks who were as into the costumed look as they were, such as Moloch the Mystic, the Screaming Skull, and the gorilla-masked King

FINAL ★★★★★ The New York Gazette. **WEATHER**

MYSTERIOUS MASKED MAN CLEANS UP WHARF

Mob. During the war, Nite Owl himself famously knocked out the Nazi agent Captain Axis.

The Cold War seemed to cast a chill over the Minutemen's activities. Members left or were forced out. Some died or disappeared. There was the harassment of the McCarthy hearings. The interesting crooks were all in jail or had moved on to less ostentatious sorts of criminal pursuits. Nobody felt like playing dress-up with them, and the remaining Minutemen started to feel a little foolish. They broke up as a group long before the appearance of a real super hero in the person of Dr. Manhattan made them truly redundant. A few continued fighting what crime they could on their own, but the Golden Age was clearly over.

Hollis retired from the police department and costumed adventuring in the early '60s, choosing instead to get a "proper job" by opening an auto repair shop like the one his father had worked in. He published his memoir, *Under the Hood*, in 1967. Some people got upset by the sordid underbelly of the hero fad he exposed in the book, but that was only because it was all too true. In it he also confesses to having, if not outright regret, at least nagging pangs of concern that by dressing up and taking the law into their own hands, they had quite possibly changed the country in fundamental ways.

Like Sally, Hollis took some joy in the fact that his legacy would be carried on by someone worthy – Dan Dreiberg. Unlike Sally, of course, Hollis hadn't trained or even recruited Dan; his reputation had been enough to inspire the young man to follow in his footsteps. The two became good friends over the years, especially after the Keene Act sidelined Dan, swapping beers and harrowing tales of yesteryear at weekly bull sessions. In fact, it was because a group of Knot-Tops mistook Hollis for the current Nite Owl that he was attacked and beaten to death one night in his apartment.

Played by Glenn Ennis

Making his debut in the fall of 1938, Hooded Justice was the first real-life masked vigilante and one of the most mysterious. A tall and powerfully muscled man, he made an imposing figure in his executioner's hood, cape, and signature noose. In his first escapade, he put three would-be muggers in the hospital, one of whom was left paralyzed from the waist down.

Hooded Justice seemed to be filled to bursting with contradictions. He voiced support for Hitler's policies before America entered the Second World War, and yet was involved in a turbulent love affair with Nelson "Nelly" Gardner (AKA Captain Metropolis) for many years – this despite often being seen in public with Silk Spectre I on his brawny arm. A big part of what made his relationship with Gardner so rocky was that Hooded Justice was reportedly often out all night with boys and was into the "rough stuff."

Despite being a staunch anti-Communist, Hooded Justice refused to testify before the House Committee on Un-American Activities since it meant he would have to reveal his identity to an official of the Committee. He disappeared soon after. There was speculation that he might have been a famous circus strongman named Rolf Müller, who went missing at about the same time. A body with a bullet in its head washed up later on a Massachusetts beach, and was tentatively identified as Müller's.

Ozymandias' investigations many years later led him to the Comedian as Hooded Justice's killer, although he could never prove it. Did the Comedian make good on his threat to get Hooded Justice in retaliation for the thrashing he received when he tried to rape Sally Jupiter? Or was it a government-ordered assassination? Even if Hooded Justice and Rolf Müller were the same person, there is evidence that the latter was purely an alias. Clearly, since anyone who might know his true identity is dead, we may never know the answer to the question: "Who was that masked man?"

A top college athlete from Kansas, Dollar Bill found employment in New York as a private masked hero for one of the major bank chains. His distinctive costume, designed especially for the bank, included a flowing red cape to increase his visibility to the public. In 1951, while he was trying to foil a robbery at one of the banks he was meant to safeguard, his cape got caught in the revolving door, rendering him helpless; he was subsequently shot in the head at close range.

DOLLAR BILL

Played by Dan Payne

SILHOUETTE

AKA Ursula Zandt, played by Apollonia Vanova

Originally an Austrian aristocrat of Jewish descent, Ursula fled her homeland with the coming of the Nazis. Once she was comfortably ensconced in New York, she took to crime fighting as a means of combating boredom. On her first outing in 1939, she busted up a child pornography ring, soundly thrashing three of the men involved. Other members of the Minutemen found her arrogant and more than a bit abrasive; Sally Jupiter never liked her personally, and Hooded Justice clashed with her over their widely divergent political views – which should come as no surprise.

When it was learned that Silhouette had been living with another woman in a lesbian relationship, Laurence Schexnayder convinced the other Minutemen to toss her out of the group in order to avert any bad publicity that exposure of her lifestyle might create. Both she and her girlfriend were brutally murdered in her apartment soon after; an old adversary known as the Liquidator was rumored to have done the deed.

A former lieutenant in the United States Marine Corps, Nelson Gardner brought military organization and strategic thinking to the battle against crime. It was he who first wrote to Sally Jupiter and suggested forming a "battalion" of costumed heroes, what eventually became the Minutemen. (He had chosen to contact her because she was the only vigilante represented by an agent with a listed address.)

Nelson was a true believer in stamping out what he perceived to be the ills of society. He also harbored racist views toward blacks and Hispanics that surprised even his contemporaries in pre-Civil Rights Movement America. Known as "Nelly" to his close associates, he was in a tumultuous homosexual relationship with Hooded Justice throughout the '40s. Given a passing grade by the House Committee on Un-American Activities due to his exemplary military service, he was an active adventurer into the '60s. He was decapitated in a car crash in 1974.

CAPTAIN METROPOLIS

AKA Nelson Gardner, played by Darryl Scheelar

MOTHMAN

AKA Byron Lewis, played by Niall Matter

A gentleman of leisure in his native Connecticut, Byron Lewis carved out a niche in the masked vigilante world by designing a costume with wings that actually allowed him to glide for short distances. He used them to swoop down on criminals and take them unawares. Apparently uncomfortable with direct confrontations, Lewis registered as a Conscientious Objector during the Second World War.

After a decade of clashing with criminals, and especially after Dollar Bill's demise at such a young age, Lewis started to hit the bottle pretty hard. The fact that he had had left-wing sympathizers as friends in his distant past did not sit well with the House Committee on Un-American Activities; they eventually cleared him of any actual disloyalty to his country, but not before putting him through hell. His drinking worsened, along with his fragile mental state, and in due time he was committed to an insane asylum in Maine.

VINTAGE VILLIANS

Capitan Axis played by Darryl Scheelar. Mobster played by Jim Ralph. Spaceman played by Garvin Cross.

A German agent during World War II, Captain Axis (left) was involved in sabotage in the New York City/tri-state area. Nite Owl I punched his lights out with a well aimed left hook. Homegrown adversaries, such as Mobster (center) and Spaceman (right), also faced off against the Minutemen throughout the 1940s.

AKA Edgar William Jacobi, played by Matt Frewer

"OH, GOD, PLEASE. I DID MY TIME. I'M NOT MOLOCH ANYMORE. WHAT DO YOU WANT FROM ME?"

Edgar Jacobi was wowing crowds in seedy nightclubs with his magic as Moloch the Mystic when he was still a teenager, but he wanted more out of life. "He's a small man with big ideas who managed to engineer them into a life of stage magic," says actor Matt Frewer. "He gained a certain notoriety in underground clubs and got in with the wrong crowd."

In the early '40s, he figured he could make more money through crime than with his penny-ante hocus pocus act. He kept the magician persona, however, for the sake of panache. He was flashy in those early years, employing devices like his 'solar mirror weapon' in his devious capers.

With time, he learned that overt crimes didn't pay as well as the impersonal kind. He transitioned into running vice-clubs, overseeing some drug dealing, and dabbling in financial fraud. Still, he occasionally found time for spectacular scores: kidnapping the Governor of New Jersey in 1964, hijacking the luxury liner *Queen Elizabeth II* in 1972, and the bombing of the New York Stock Exchange in 1977. Over the years, Moloch ran afoul of several costumed vigilantes out to make names for themselves. Dr. Manhattan disintegrated several of Moloch's top lieutenants and trigger-men in the '60s, and it took all his guile to stay one step ahead of the Comedian during a rivalry that lasted over twenty years.

Opposite: Moloch the Mystic at the height of his powers.

Above: Edgar Jacobi receives a visit from an old adversary.

Below right: The Comedian unburdens himself.

Opposite: Jacobi as Rorschach finds him on his second visit.

Eventually his luck ran out. Moloch went to prison for some minor crime, but he found Jesus inside the joint. Attempting to go straight when he got out, he was only too happy to take a job at Pyramid Transnational when they unexpectedly recruited him. He could only afford a shabby apartment in a shabbier neighborhood – nothing like his former glory days with every comfort and desire at his fingertips – but at least he was making amends and an honest living.

But, then came the cancer. Then the Comedian surprised him in the middle of the night, whimpering like a little girl and blabbering about some list. Finally, Rorschach paid him a visit that was less than social. Can't a former super-villain just live out what's left of his life in peace?

In a lot of ways, Moloch can be seen as the opposite number from Hollis Mason. He's given up the life and has his eyes on the future, one day at a time, while Hollis is more entrenched in reliving his memories, at least in his mind. "Moloch is ready to leave it behind," says Frewer. "We were pretty careful not to have posters of his time as a magician up in his apartment, for instance. He's distanced himself from it, whereas Hollis, I think, is still harboring nostalgia." Moloch may not want to be dragged back into the fray, but what he just doesn't realize is, he never left it.

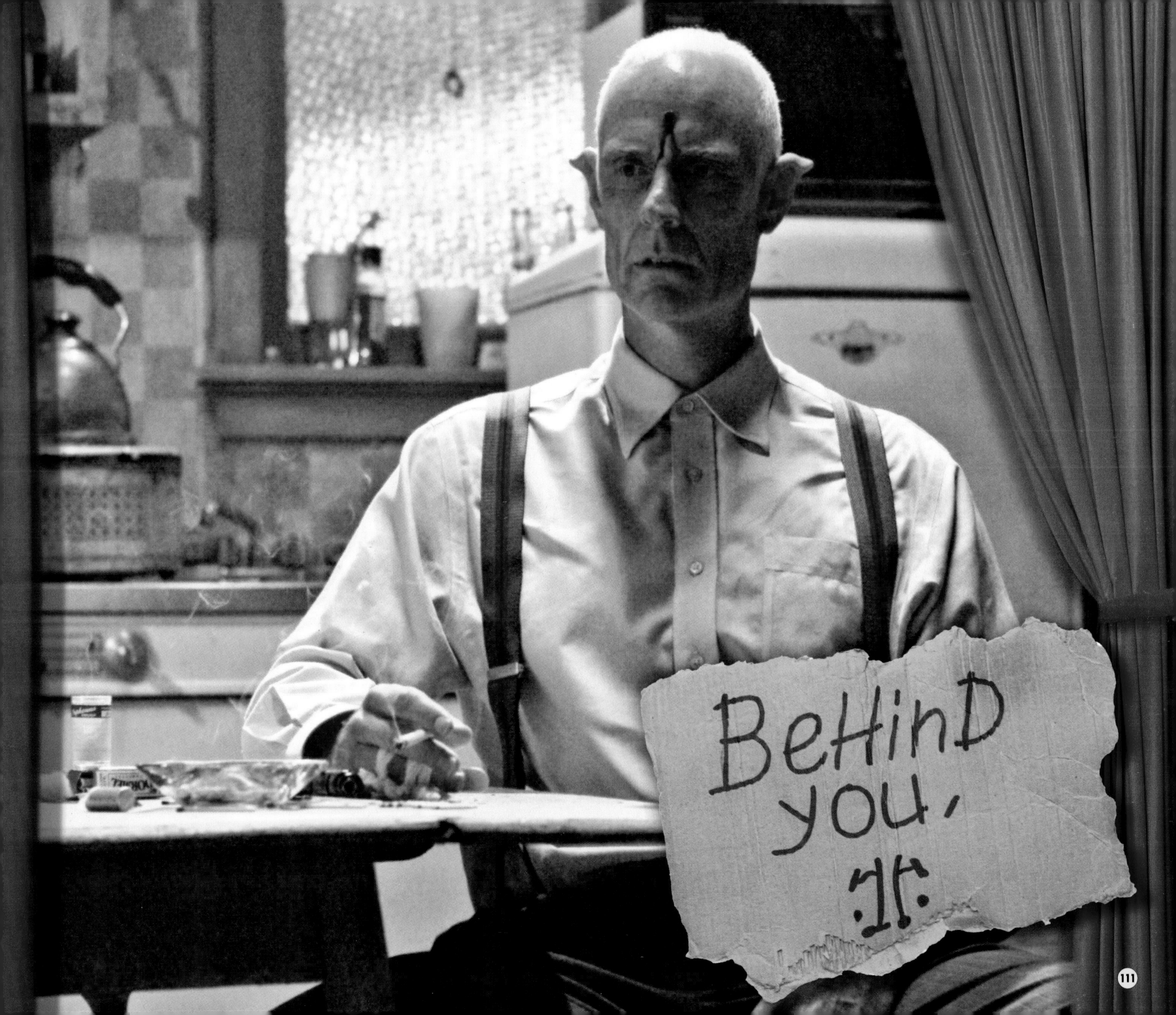
BeHinD
you,

KNOT-TOPS

The name refers both to members of a prominent youth gang as well as the samurai-like hairstyle they sport. Their hairdos and manner of dress have permeated the country's urban culture, and have been imitated by other teens and young adults with no gang affiliations. Disaffected and nihilistic, hardcore Knot-Tops scoff at society and indulge in street drugs like KT-28s ('Katies'). Self-appointed authority figures like costumed vigilantes are special objects of loathing for them. A group of Knot-Tops beat Hollis Mason to death, mistakenly thinking he was the newly reactivated Nite Owl II.

BIG FIGURE

Played by Danny Woodburn

"THERE ARE MORE THAN FIFTY PEOPLE IN HERE THAT YOU PUT AWAY... THEY'RE ALL DYING TO GET A PIECE OF YOU. THIS PLACE IS GONNA EXPLODE. THEN YOU DIE BY INCHES."

Big Figure was a powerful presence in the New York City underworld, heading up a sizable organized crime syndicate for most of the 1960s. In 1970, Nite Owl II and Rorschach smashed his mob and put the diminutive crime lord away in Sing Sing for an extended cooling-off period.

On Halloween Night 1985, during a prison riot sparked by the death of an inmate at the hands of then-incarcerated Rorschach, Big Figure and two compatriots attempted to exact revenge on his old nemesis. They were unsuccessful to say the least.

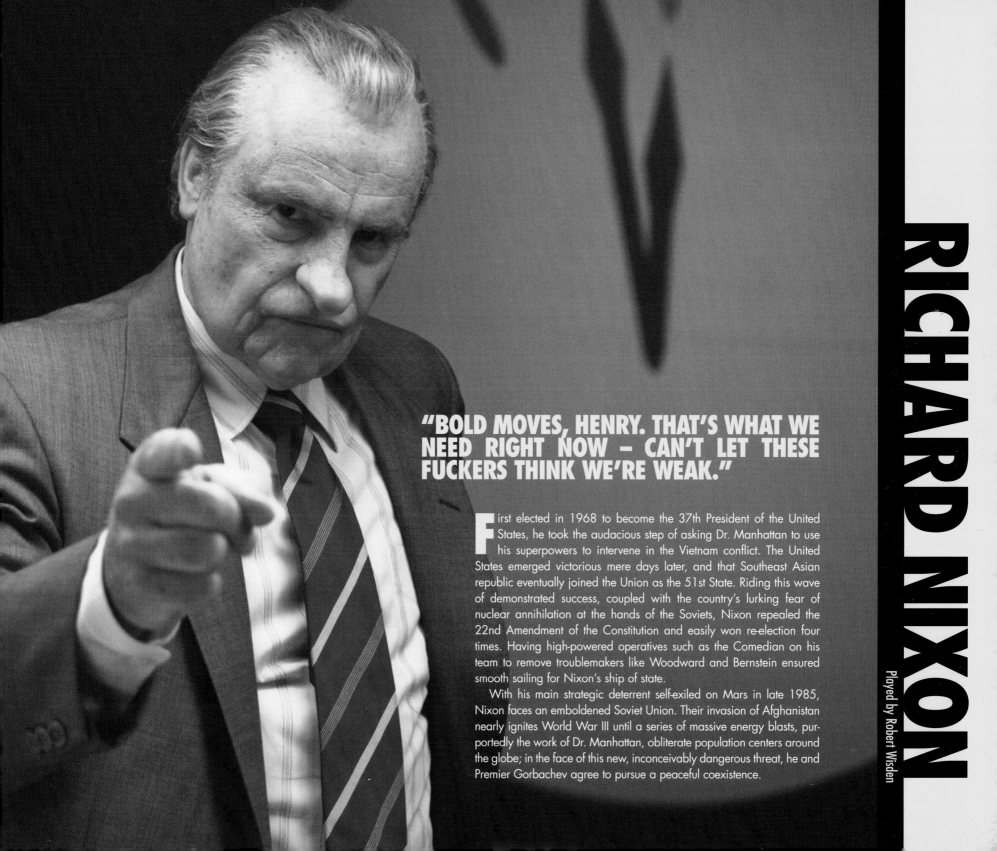

RICHARD NIXON

Played by Robert Wisden

"BOLD MOVES, HENRY. THAT'S WHAT WE NEED RIGHT NOW – CAN'T LET THESE FUCKERS THINK WE'RE WEAK."

First elected in 1968 to become the 37th President of the United States, he took the audacious step of asking Dr. Manhattan to use his superpowers to intervene in the Vietnam conflict. The United States emerged victorious mere days later, and that Southeast Asian republic eventually joined the Union as the 51st State. Riding this wave of demonstrated success, coupled with the country's lurking fear of nuclear annihilation at the hands of the Soviets, Nixon repealed the 22nd Amendment of the Constitution and easily won re-election four times. Having high-powered operatives such as the Comedian on his team to remove troublemakers like Woodward and Bernstein ensured smooth sailing for Nixon's ship of state.

With his main strategic deterrent self-exiled on Mars in late 1985, Nixon faces an emboldened Soviet Union. Their invasion of Afghanistan nearly ignites World War III until a series of massive energy blasts, purportedly the work of Dr. Manhattan, obliterate population centers around the globe; in the face of this new, inconceivably dangerous threat, he and Premier Gorbachev agree to pursue a peaceful coexistence.

"WHO MAKES THE WORLD?"
– DR. MANHATTAN

PRODUCTION

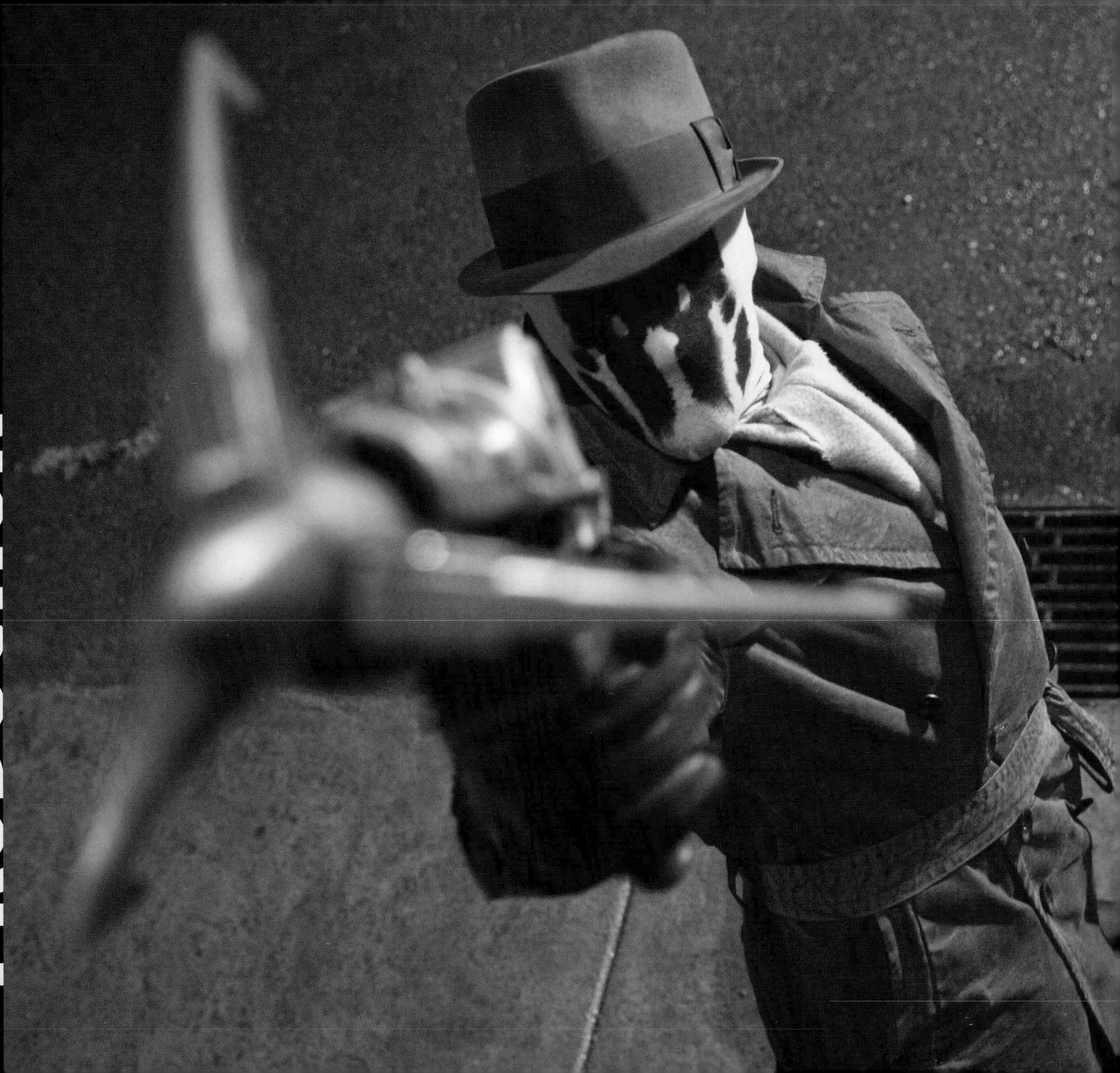

FILMING THE UNFILMABLE

The full cast and crew assembled in Vancouver in the late summer of 2007 for rehearsals and camera tests. Everyone, from the producers to the production assistants, was feeling the pressure to live up to the legacy of the graphic novel, but probably no one more than Zack Snyder. "We loved the book," he says, "and we loved the images, and we really cared to make them come to life as much as we could, and make it respectful." Or, as he reportedly told studio executives months earlier, "If I fuck this up, I might as well start making romantic comedies!"

For the actors playing the masked heroes, even after months of fight training and the hours it took each day to get into costume and make-up, many still found the scope of the production exciting, daunting, and even a bit surreal. "The passion – I've never seen any group of people so passionate about a project, ever. It is intimidating, I'm not going to lie," says Jeffrey Dean Morgan, and then adds with a grin, "The Comedian is *not* intimidated. Jeffrey Dean Morgan's a little intimidated."

For his part, Patrick Wilson found Nite Owl's suit a bit stiff, but he took it in his stride. "It's high class problems, I like to say. What am I going to do, complain about being in the suit?" asks Wilson. "Yeah, I'm not going to complain about the suit. Every day I got in that suit, man, was just like a gift. It's pretty cool." Jackie Earle Haley recalls reuniting with Wilson, his co-star from *Little Children*, under these very different circumstances: "We were doing our first scene together. It was in Veidt's place… We get there and we're looking around. There I am in my sock [mask]. There he is in his goggles. And I go, 'Who would've guessed this shit about two years ago?' We started laughing."

Although few of the actors had even read the graphic novel when they signed on, by the time shooting began they were all true believers. The book became like a sacred text to be studied and lived; its words and images informed how they approached their characters and added to the shared vision being created. "The cast has been super awesome at helping me at every turn," says Snyder. "They read the graphic novel every day. A lot of times they'll go, 'Yeah, but my character says this. See this little circle by his head? That's what he says.'"

From the first table read, Malin Akerman knew she was part of an extraordinary ensemble. "Every single person is really invested in this project, and I think that makes all the difference," she says. "Everyone's done their research, and is really excited, and I think that translates into the characters. Everyone goes into it with such ease, and you go, 'How is this possible that everyone *is* their character?' I think a little bit of magic just happened with this film, absolutely."

Opposite: Veidt confronts Blake, and Rorschach inspects the aftermath (the mask was added in post-production).

Above: Matthew Goode and Malin Akerman get styled.
Above right: Zack Snyder checks a shot.

Principal photography commenced on September 17, 2007– nearly twenty years to the day after the final issue of the comic book series appeared. Like the original creators, Snyder had a different way of doing things, his own idiosyncratic methods for capturing the very specific images and performances he desired.

For example, ninety percent of the time only one camera was rolling during any shot – an unusual choice in these days of multiple camera set-ups. "When you make a movie, a lot of times when the actors are talking you stick a second camera in there to try to get a close up or something to make it move along faster, 'cause you get a free second angle that's a bit tighter," explains Snyder. "The problem we faced was that second camera normally suffers a bit in its composition and design, just because it's not the primary focus. Sometimes it's not a big deal, sometimes maybe it's better to have that kind of off angle, but not for this movie."

Below: Veidt, his assistant, and Dan attend Edward Blake's funeral.

Opposite: Rorschach pays his final respects to the Comedian after hours.

THE SHOOT

Like Dr. Manhattan, however, Snyder couldn't be everywhere at once. A second camera, run by gifted filmmaker Bill Dalgleish, ran on many of the stunts as well as the inserts of important elements. "Bill's whole unit is pretty much photographing the details of *Watchmen*, like the close-ups of the [smiley face] button," says Snyder. Dalgleish consulted closely with editor William Hoy along with Snyder to determine the necessary shots for expounding on the storyline.

It's a normal approach to filmmaking that movies are often shot wildly out of order. In striving for maximum efficiency, all scenes that take place on a certain set would be filmed together; similarly for all shots on a set that face in the same direction. While this saves time (and time is money), the cast and crew need to keep meticulous track of props, costumes, and make-up to prevent egregious continuity errors between scenes that are chronologically adjacent but filmed weeks apart. Likewise, the actors can be stressed by getting into the proper frame of mind for their characters – often having to react to something that happened long ago, or hasn't happened yet.

Snyder, on the other hand, prefers to minimize those particular difficulties and shoot in the order of the script and his storyboards as much as possible. The storyboards, in fact, accompany him to the set, and

miniature versions detailing the day's shooting are distributed to the crew. "I've only done three movies, so those three movies we've shot pretty much from beginning to end each time. That can be a problem for production, but they try and accommodate me," he says.

The producers seemed to get it. "The last thing I want to do is sit there and say, 'We're not being efficient here. Let's shoot everything in this direction. Let's put three cameras on and then we can turn around,'" says executive producer Herb Gains. "Then what you're doing is you're shooting a schedule, you're not shooting a movie, number one; number two, if the director is not in his comfort zone, then you're not saving time at the end of the day. You run the risk of something being missed, something falling through the cracks, losing a shot, or performances being whacked out, and having to go in and re-shoot."

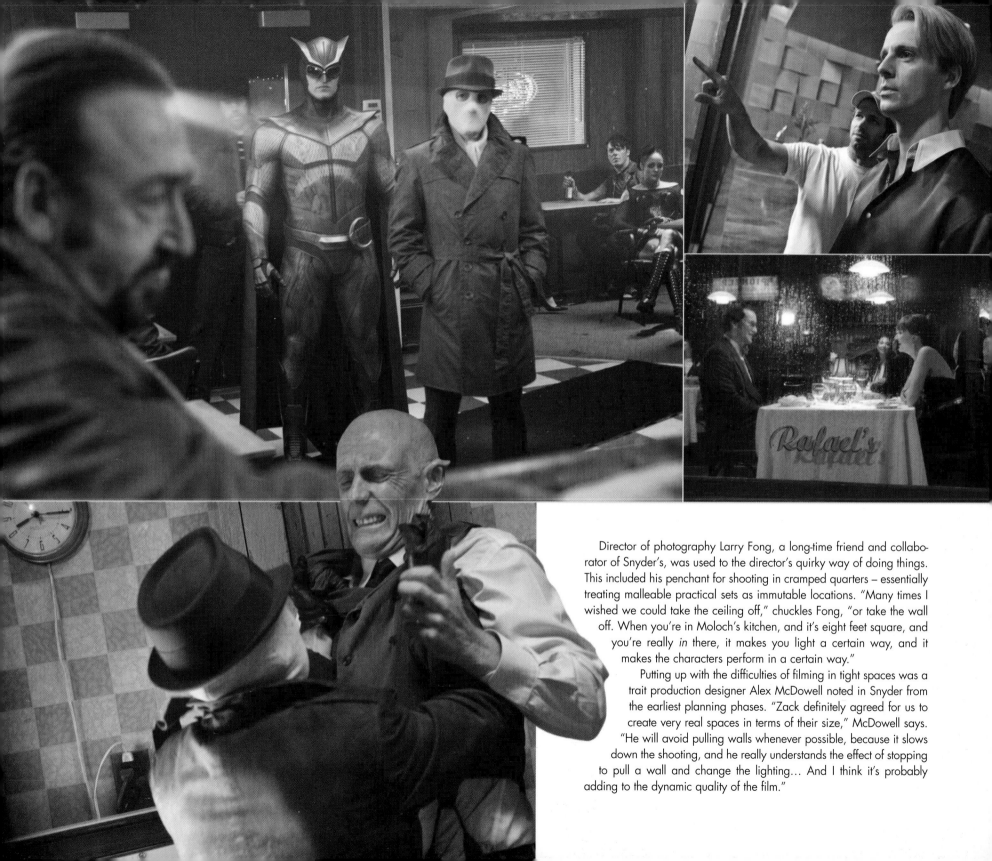

Director of photography Larry Fong, a long-time friend and collaborator of Snyder's, was used to the director's quirky way of doing things. This included his penchant for shooting in cramped quarters – essentially treating malleable practical sets as immutable locations. "Many times I wished we could take the ceiling off," chuckles Fong, "or take the wall off. When you're in Moloch's kitchen, and it's eight feet square, and you're really *in* there, it makes you light a certain way, and it makes the characters perform in a certain way."

Putting up with the difficulties of filming in tight spaces was a trait production designer Alex McDowell noted in Snyder from the earliest planning phases. "Zack definitely agreed for us to create very real spaces in terms of their size," McDowell says. "He will avoid pulling walls whenever possible, because it slows down the shooting, and he really understands the effect of stopping to pull a wall and change the lighting… And I think it's probably adding to the dynamic quality of the film."

OWLSHIP

One of the tightest spaces in the whole shoot was the interior of Archie, Nite Owl's Owlship. Oftentimes with a vehicle like that, film-makers will "cheat" by building a slightly larger interior to facilitate filming. With Archie, however, so much of the ship's interior was visible through the large windshields that the audience would detect such a trick. Therefore, in the end, a single Owlship was constructed for both interior and exterior shots.

"There was constant paranoia and nervousness about the safety of the Owlship," recalls McDowell, "suspending it above the crowd, and only building one. Everyone always freaks out about not having a back-up." He conjectured, however, that Archie and any passengers could have survived quite a drop, as former custom yacht builder, Jack Gauvreau, had built the ship very solidly out of steel, wood, and fiberglass to exacting specifications.

STUNTS

Safety, of course, was always the foremost concern during any of the stunt work. While not a conventional action film by any stretch of the imagination, *Watchmen* contains several scenes where acts of violence are essential to the narrative. "I don't think it's full of what you would classically call action," says Snyder, "but it's full of spectacle. There are certainly action sequences in the movie, but they're operatic. They're designed to tell a certain, specific story."

Stunt coordinator and fight choreographer Damon Caro admits there was a fine line to walk. "It was a lot of meetings, bouncing stuff around about how much to elaborate the fight scenes, trying to stay true to the novel, but amplifying all the action for a film." From tons of wire work to bone-breaking punches, to a flame-throwing aerosol can, to a gel burn on bare flesh, Caro had his work cut out for him.

In addition to his own crew, Caro put the actors through weeks of physical training and fight blocking, because part of using violence to tell a story meant striving to be as real as possible. Akerman says that even *appearing* to fight like Silk Spectre II took plenty of time and perseverance. "The stunt coordinator and his team do things, and it looks amazing," she recalls. "When you try to do it, and you look at yourself in the mirror trying to look like a fighter, you look like a ballerina trying to look like a fighter. It was really frustrating." If her fight sequences in the alley, in the prison riot, and at Karnak are any indication, it would seem she got the hang of it.

Haley came to the role of Rorschach with probably the most fight experience of any of the actors, which proved to be ironic. Caro explains, "I looked at his movement and his martial arts ability, and I go, 'That's awesome. Too bad that's the one guy I have who wears a mask.' He needed the least amount of work, but I can double him the easiest."

This spread: Patrick Wilson and Malin Akerman undergo extensive fight training to play retired super heroes. They use it with devastating effect in the alley (opposite bottom and below left) and during the prison riot (below).

Above: An inmate catches fire in the first ever bare-skin burn in a feature film.

Below: Rorschach torches the SWAT team.

This page: Rorschach leaps from Moloch's apartment into the arms of the NYPD.

Opposite: Rorschach reminds the cons who's in charge.

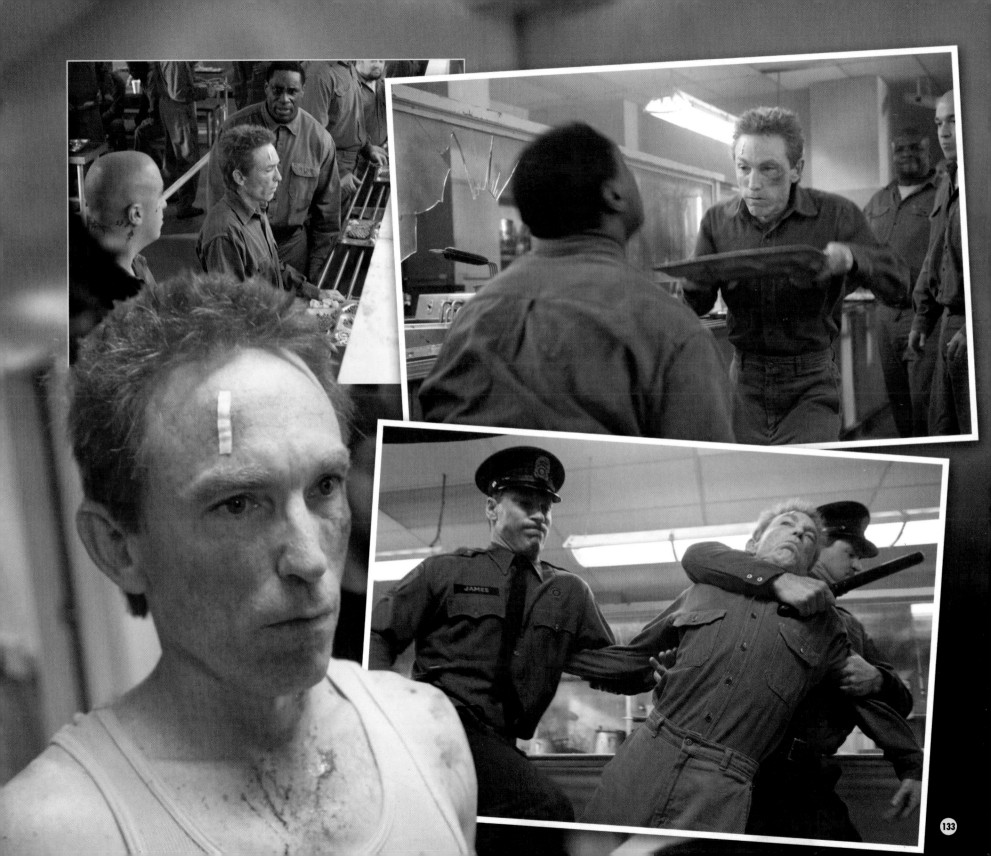

THE ARTIST ON SET

Probably the most memorable time during the entire production for everyone was the visit to set by Dave Gibbons. The artist toured the backlot and soundstages, sat in on some filming, watched some shot footage, and signed autographs for the cast and crew – oh, and he was mightily impressed by the passion, commitment, and utmost attention to detail he witnessed.

"There's a lot of pressure," says Fong. "Everyone knows the *Watchmen* story, and so many people have tried it, and it hasn't happened. So, for Dave Gibbons to come to the set, and to see how thrilled he was, that's encouraging for us to know. 'Wow. Okay, I think we're not going to screw it up.'"

"This was the moment of truth," producer Lloyd Levin explains. "After all this time and effort, was the movie being done right? And Dave's total joy in seeing Zack and crew's realization for the film was a great relief to all." The eagle-eyed among the audience can look for Gibbon's trademark "G" among the tangle of graffiti on the streets of New York – a nod that the artist has signed off on the project.

Opposite left: Stuntman Rich Cetrone teaches Jeffrey Dean Morgan to kick some ass. **Opposite right:** He puts it to good use.

Below: Dave Gibbons' blessing adorns a light pole.

A great deal of the credit has to go to Snyder, not just for his creative vision, but also for his unflagging energy that infused and motivated the whole production team. "He's got an unbelievable enthusiasm about what he's doing," says McDowell. "It's completely infectious to work around him in terms of maintaining that degree of enthusiasm. He's got a wonderful respect for all of the crew, so that everybody is engaged and wants to do exactly what it is that he wants to see. He has the confidence to remain focused on the story, and allow each of us to do what we've been hired to do."

Snyder's ability to focus owes a great debt to his wife and producer, Deborah, who is a true force of nature behind the scenes. "In all my years, I've never seen a more competent team than Zack and Debbie," explains producer Larry Gordon. "They complement each other in every way and are great collaborators." And on a shoot of this scale, lasting 101 days through a Vancouver winter, those were vital qualities to have.

Above: Zack and Deborah Snyder on set with Producer Larry Gordon.
Right: Producer Lloyd Levin (left) on set with Zack Snyder.

Opposite: Jeffrey Dean Morgan gets his copy of *Absolute Watchmen* signed by its artist.

DAVE GIBBONS' SET REPORT

It's perhaps the most surreal experience of my life.

There they are, in a shadowy clubhouse, standing around a map of the USA, just as we'd imagined them. The smoke of the Comedian's cigar hangs in the air as I drink in the details of the scene. Framed old copies of *The New York Gazette* tell stories of past exploits; trophies glint in glass-fronted display cases; Moloch's solar weapon shines in a dusty corner and over there, on its mannequin stand, the faded costume of the original Nite Owl keeps silent vigil.

Then, a sudden flash of unearthly blue light announces the arrival of Dr. Manhattan and the tableau comes to life. The voices of quarreling heroes rise and fall, a Zippo flares and the map catches fire.

Somewhere, someone shouts "Cut!"

And I'm standing amongst them. Nite Owl shakes my hand. The Comedian slaps me on the back. Silk Spectre smiles a dazzling greeting. I'm overwhelmed by the depth and detail of what I'm seeing.

But more than that. I'm overwhelmed by the commitment, the passion, the palpable desire to do this right.

I'm starting to feel a glow that eclipses even Dr. Manhattan's…

On the movie backlot, like a sailor on shore leave, I gawp in wonder at a New York City that never really was. Once a Canadian lumber yard, it's become a complex of American city streets.

At the corner, a Treasure Island store promises a bounty of pulp thrills; down the block, the Gunga Diner beckons, fully fitted out in chrome and purple leather and, over there, the Rumrunner sign looms luridly. Even the austere façade of the Institute for Extraspatial Studies can't spoil the gaudy fun.

On an upper floor, I spot the windows of the Judomaster Martial Arts Studio. I'm stopped in my tracks. Judomaster? Detail piles on dizzying detail.

Rain's falling hard now and I'm led inside, through a grubby little hovel crammed with dressmaking dummies, past the huge halls of Karnak, into Dan Dreiberg's homely brownstone and down to where the Owlship sits. I clamber aboard in giddy delight.

The rest of the visit kaleidoscopes crazily by: I watch footage of Rorschach pulling Nite Owl off a bloodied Knot Top; I flip through an issue of the Black Freighter; on a laptop, I see raw CGI blocking for the Vietnam sequence; I hold a smiley face pin splattered with what looks like real human bean juice; sitting in my own personal director's chair, I sign dozens of books and posters for cast and crew…

Finally, tired but happy, arms around my new buddies, costumed and otherwise, it's my turn to smile for the camera.

A month later, I'm smiling still.

From the online movie production blog, December 2007

CHAPTER V

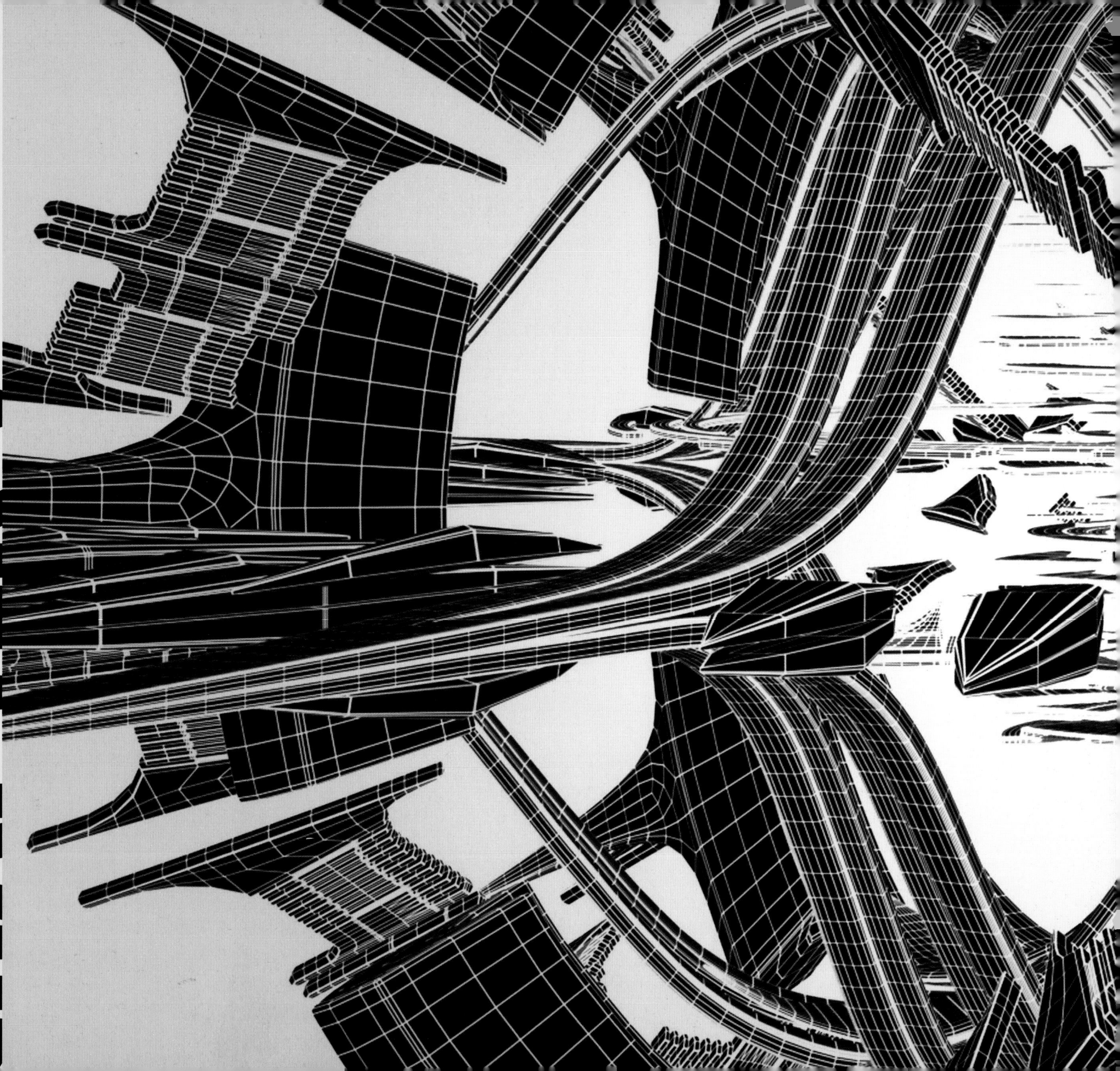

"TO DISTILL SO SPECIFIC A FORM FROM ALL OF THAT CHAOS..."
– DR. MANHATTAN

The term 'post-production' is really a bit of a misnomer. Key personnel responsible for the final visual effects on the film, for example, were involved from the earliest planning stages. The editorial crew had cutting rooms set up in Burnaby, British Columbia before filming commenced, and they began piecing together shots on Day Two. Of course, everyone in post was also looking at perhaps another year of work after the last piece of film had been exposed. "When everybody's wrapped here and they feel like they can sleep now, that's when I have to hit it even harder," says the film's editor, William Hoy.

Like the folks on the production side, the members of the post-production crew were appreciative of the enormous amounts of detailed preparation that Snyder and the art department worked out ahead of time. It made working on such an intricate film that much easier and certainly more enjoyable. Hoy, who has worked with Snyder twice before, notes the director storyboarded *Watchmen* more completely than either of his two previous films. "I

think this one was very complicated for everybody involved," Hoy says, "and I think he wanted to at least lay it out for people."

Visual effects (VFX) supervisor John 'D. J.' DesJardin found having the groundwork laid beforehand to be a refreshing change from some of his previous film experiences. "You're working on a movie where people just don't have any idea what they want to do. Guys like me become the fallback, you know? 'We'll fix it all later. We'll figure it out later. Just shoot everything every way you can do it, and we'll put it together later,'" he laughs. "It's nice to walk into a situation where Zack shows me these boards in January [2007] and says, 'This is how I want to start the movie.' And you're really psyched by what you see, and your mind starts going, 'Well, how are we going to do this, that, and the other thing?'"

Making collaborative choices early on helped get the pipeline flowing that much quicker. "Zack, since he is very decisive in making this movie, was already able to turn over shots as far back as the second

week," recalls DesJardin. Turning over shots meant that Snyder and Hoy were confident that a certain take would be used in the final film, and the VFX department was free to set off down the long road of working on it to make it perfect. Starting from temporary effects to get an idea of how the shot should look, narrowing down and refining that look to the final, polished version, can easily take three months for a few seconds of screen time.

Despite the head start, the period during filming was only a warm-up for VFX. "Once we get done here, it'll start in earnest. I can focus all my time and energy on getting all of that stuff going and done, because suddenly we'll have hundreds of shots in play," says DesJardin. "There are other miniature elements that have to be shot for the tenement fire. We've been in development on Mars, but we have to turn it into 3-D elements. It's kind of endless." Helping out were a host of vendors, including Sony Image Works, MPC, CIS, Intelligent Creatures, and New Deal.

Previous spread: The Mars palace takes shape, from 3-D wireframe to final shot.

This spread: Viet Cong surrender to Dr. Manhattan in a concept sketch (left), during principle photography (opposite), and in the finished shot (above).

RORSCHACH'S MASK

One of the trickier effects to create was the ever-changing pattern of Rorschach's mask. Actor Jackie Earle Haley wore a special balaclava that gave his head a distinctly round shape, but exposed his eyes and eyebrows to show his expression. His mouth remained covered, but markers on the mask allowed its movements to be digitally traced. "He wears that, he emotes," explains DesJardin, "and then we take it back to the shop and replace everything on the face with a CG version of the texture and the blots moving around according to his performance."

DesJardin goes on to point out that the inkblot patterns had to be created wholly in-house, as the ones from the original Rorschach Test are copyrighted. "There are set patterns that we defined as expressions. There's fifteen of them," he says. "It's up to whatever Zack thinks it ought to be for whatever expression. So if he's astonished, it's pattern ten; if he's kind of sad, maybe it's pattern twelve." An animator hand drew interesting shapes as key frames in between the patterns, and then software was used to animate the blots between those shapes. Detailed edge treatment and precise speed control made it

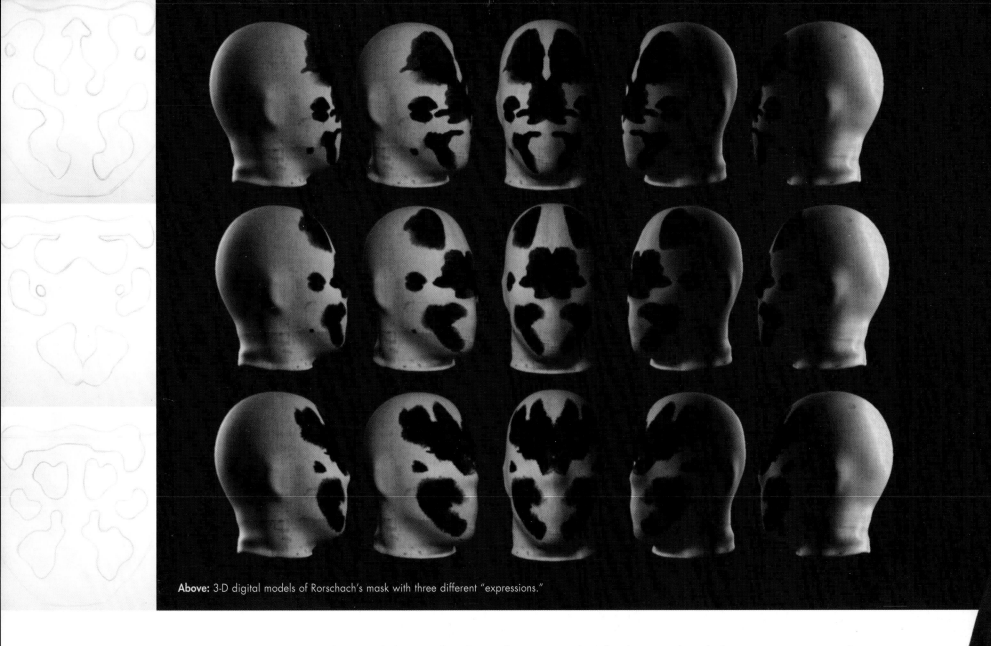

Above: 3-D digital models of Rorschach's mask with three different "expressions."

Paying meticulous attention the myriad elements of each VFX shot, however, was never about spectacle simply for spectacle's sake. "We're trying to cram as much of these little esoteric details in there as we can so that it becomes a real psychological, emotional, spiritual journey," explains DesJardin. "If it's not, then it's just action. The meaning of it is gone. And nobody working on it wants it to be that."

Hoy shares this sentiment, although he admits that working on a film based on a well-known graphic novel sometimes adds an extra level of challenge for an editor. "I've worked on pictures where you pretty much

have freedom to work in whichever way you want," explains Hoy. "You get to the end and go, 'It's not working.' So, what do you do? Let's make it a flashback, or let's make it a dream, or let's make the good guy the bad guy. But you wouldn't want to do that in a graphic novel, especially *Watchmen*." He adds, laughing, "That would be blasphemous."

Getting specific images perfectly right on film so they have the same emotional punch as in the original material is critical in a movie of this nature. "There are certain iconic frames that we have to stay true to, frames that relate back to the graphic novel," Hoy says. And he knows

whereof he speaks, having cut *300*, which was based on the stunning work by Frank Miller. "In *300* there were some frames we tried to maximize – say, when the king is going up the cliff to visit the Ephors and he's jumping – we would slow it down just as he reached for the cliff and his cape flew out, just like in the graphic novel," Hoy recalls.

Watchmen provided many such moments that needed to be savored onscreen: the Comedian crashing through the window of his high-rise apartment to the street below, with the smiley-face button fluttering down after him; Dr. Manhattan striding unchallenged through the rice paddies of Vietnam, dispassionately disintegrating his foes; the clockwork glass palace rising from the surface of Mars. "It's those kind of frames you want to just burn into the viewer's mind, without being disruptive to the story," says Hoy.

But he adds this caveat: "You can have as many iconic moments as you want, but if you don't care about the characters, you're not going to care about the film." A big part of why we care about the characters in *Watchmen* is that they are such flawed heroes. One of Hoy's jobs as editor was to bring those flaws to light by recognizing and emphasizing nuances in the actors' performances that pointed out this duality. Oftentimes, these were moments never mentioned in the script.

As an example, Hoy points out a scene where Nite Owl watches Rorschach roughing up a bar patron to get some information. "The actor, Patrick Wilson, gave us a couple of looks of, 'Ugh, there he goes again.' Later on, in the same scene, Nite Owl sees that his friend, Hollis Mason, has been killed by this gang. There's a Knot-Top guy in the bar, and he basically descends into hell. He just starts beating this guy worse than Rorschach ever would. First he's disapproving of it – now he just did the same thing, only worse. It's easy to miss those little looks, but those are what I try to find in a scene."

At the end of principal photography, Hoy had two weeks to complete his cut of the film. As he had been keeping up with integrating footage as it came in, and as Snyder had been reviewing the steadily growing assembly, those two weeks were really about fine tuning a known quantity. After that, Snyder sat down with Hoy for the ten-week director's cut to work out the smaller issues. "Are we too long here? How can we help this moment? That moment's great, maybe we don't need this," Hoy explains, adding, "I think of an editor as more like marathon guys. We just kind of pace ourselves. We can't be sprinting all the time because we'll never make it to the finish line."

Of course, that doesn't mean that the rest of the post-production team got to sit around on their hands while he did all the work. "While I'm working on the picture, refining it for those weeks, we're going to be putting in temporary visual effects," says Hoy. Temporary visual effects help preview audiences watching the director's cut to envision the final product. "We don't want to show the picture with green screen or Billy Crudup in an LED suit," Hoy points out.

Left: The arch-vigilante comes to life.

SOUND AND MUSIC

Below: Nite Owl II and Rorschach ransack Veidt's office (located in midtown Manhattan with the help of green screens).

Two departments whose jobs kicked into a higher gear once post started were sound and music. These are two aspects of the production that can aid in the storytelling process by immersing the audience into the emotional reality of a scene. Together they move the film into another realm frankly unattainable by the graphic novel.

Supervising sound editor Scott Hecker had collaborated with Snyder on both *Dawn of the Dead* and *300*, so they had already developed a fluid working relationship. "This being our third outing, we have the advantage of knowing how the process rolls and what's comfortable for Zack," says Hecker. "We don't have to over-communicate about what we're going to do on a given day or how

we're going to approach the project." He adds with a chuckle, "It's fun with Zack, because you rarely can be accused of going over the top."

Prep for the sound-editing team started during shooting, studying the graphic novel and even the production blog on the film's website, in order to understand some of the sonic challenges they would face. The sheer variety of creative environments in the film, as well as its overall length, presented a daunting task. "It's what I call, sound-wise and story-wise, a kaleidoscope," explains Hecker. "There's so many wildly different facets of this film, it really covers every type of sound you can imagine."

From door slams to energy blasts, every sound could stand some

tuning. "If it's not there, we add it – and if it is there, we sweeten it. We're covering everything 100%. Every single sound, even if it's good in production," Hecker points out. For example, they needed to vary the sound of face hits during a fight to keep them interesting, but they always needed to remain believable. As each costumed adventurer moved, it was essential that their outfit – whether it was made from latex, or it included a cape – sounded distinct, so that one could almost identify who's who onscreen, even while blindfolded.

Many sounds came from commercially available digital libraries, but even these needed to be bent, manipulated, phase shifted, combined, even reversed; this experimentation produced new sounds to generate just the right mood at just the right moment. It was all part of what Hecker terms, "playing in the sonic sandbox." For sounds that quite simply did not yet exist, the team ended up spending twenty-two days on a Foley stage creating them from scratch.

Certain sound constructions were months in the making, due to being linked to VFX work that was always progressing. For example, as the movements of the Owlship reached their final form, Hecker and crew got a better handle on what sound elements were needed: an air-brake opening here, a thruster pulsing there, etc. Similarly, Dr. Manhattan's clockwork glass palace on Mars went through multiple versions, each slightly different than the last; the challenge was to develop the subtle chiming of its myriad parts so that it synchronized precisely with the movement, while at the same time not interfering with the dialogue.

HEARING MANHATTAN

An intriguing bit of sound design was undertaken to give Dr. Manhattan his own sonic presence. "He's in touch with human emotions, as far removed from being a human as he ends up being, so we're trying to convey that through sound," explains Hecker. "We've done various treatments with different whale sounds, because the way they communicate underwater – it does convey emotion – whether it pitches up in frequency or goes down, becoming more mournful." He admits it is not something that many would have thought to do. "We're really trying to go above the bar and challenge ourselves to come up with stuff that people haven't heard before."

Another veteran of Snyder projects, composer Tyler Bates describes his involvement with the film as, "early and long." He began thinking about musical themes as soon as the script was approved. He also visited the set to get a sense of the characters and to grasp how Snyder felt the film was progressing. This afforded him the time to work on things, try things out, and even change directions, if needed, before tackling writing the score for the director's cut all at once.

Watchmen, with its complex storyline, interconnectivity of the various characters, and frequent swings of time and location, presented Bates with a unique challenge to treat all that musically and still make it as seamless as possible. The score was largely orchestral and choral, producing an ambience that was very ethereal and charged with emotion. "*Watchmen* is a cast of fractured characters. The music of the film reflects the loneliness each of these people has in the core of their soul, and yet there is the common bond between them, however tortured it is. That's the goal of the music – to express that," Bates says.

He saw the characters as fragments to connect and make up a whole, and so eschewed the idea of giving each individual a starkly distinct theme, while still differentiating between them. "It's not as simple as just humming a tune for this character or that character; it's more of a feeling for each of them," explains Bates. "Overall, there's a very unified, identifiable sound to the movie."

The same was true even during the film's many flashbacks. "Oftentimes when we're in a modern-day setting and we flashback to years before, the orchestration of the music changes slightly – enough to reinforce that flashback without being overtly manipulative," Bates says, and gives an example: "Perhaps where I might not be featuring woodwinds, I might introduce woodwinds to the flashback, because it just makes the music feel a little warmer and homier."

By far the most challenging part of the film to compose for was the sequence where Jon Osterman was reborn as Dr. Manhattan. "It's really intense and fantastic. It deserves great music," says Bates, wanting to take his time with the section to make sure the composition lives up to the stunning visuals. "That's one of the last things I'm touching on; I really wanted to know the movie emotionally before approaching that piece. I wanted to make sure I had the fiber of the film."

In addition to the music composed specifically for the movie, the filmmakers incorporated several well-known hits that they felt were particularly evocative of specific times and moods – everything from Nat King Cole's nostalgic "Unforgettable" to Nena's Cold War anthem "99 Luftballons." Most notable was the inclusion of Bob Dylan's classic "The Times They Are A-Changin'," which was re-recorded especially for the alternate-history montage during the opening credits.

The juxtaposition of familiar songs and unfamiliar imagery was meant purposefully to jar the audience out of its own world and into the slightly askew *Watchmen* universe. "You hear a song on oldies radio and you remember exactly where you were or what you were doing when you first heard the song," explains Hoy, "but now you're looking at these new images and it's, 'Wow, something like that could've happened.' Life could've changed, and we'd be listening to these songs under different circumstances and having different memories."

This spread: Dan and Laurie tackle the tenement fire from the Owlship.

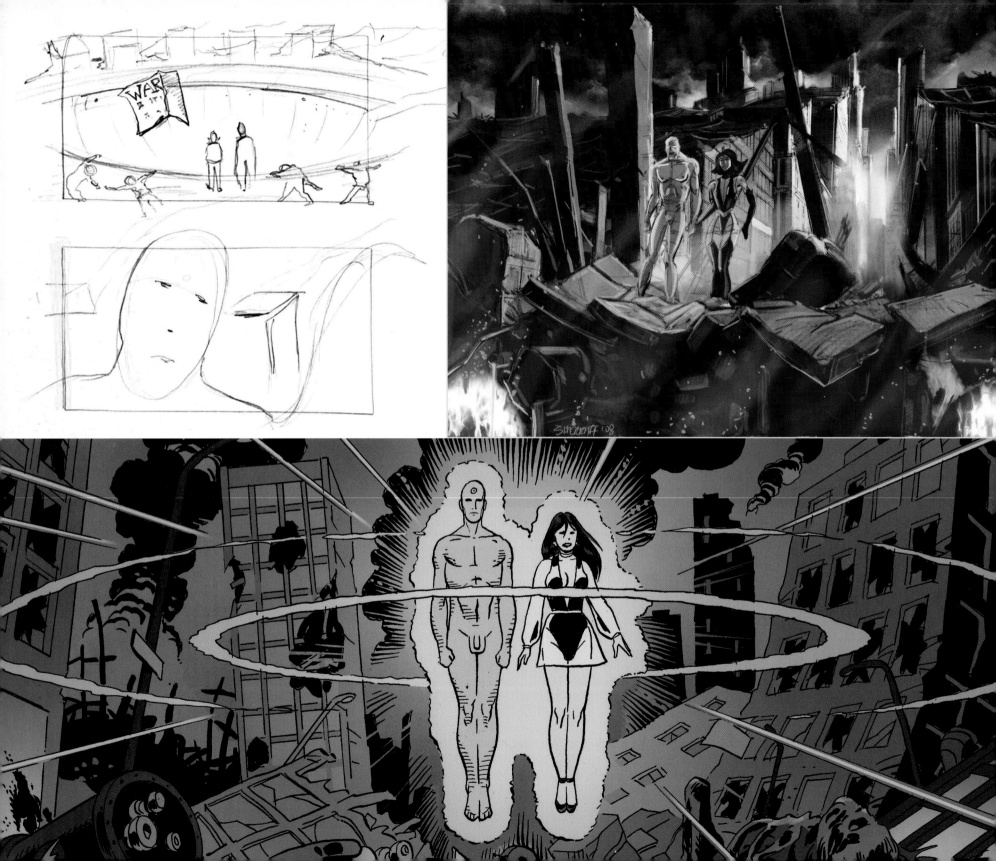

Dr. Manhattan and Laurie return to a devastated New York, as seen in (clockwise from opposite bottom) Dave Gibbons' pre-production drawing, Zack Snyder's storyboards, concept art, raw footage, and finished shot.

CHAPTER VI

"GOD EXISTS AND HE'S AMERICAN."
– WALLY WEAVER

MAKING MANHATTAN

In making a film about super heroes who are imperfect humans in a very real world, the filmmakers faced a test in bringing to the screen a super hero who was not only a godlike being, but who was also losing his humanity – and yet he had to inhabit that same real world. Dr. Manhattan needed to have an awe-inspiring presence, and at the same time interact seamlessly with the environment and people around him.

Some of the early ideas that were explored for giving this super-human character life, such as painting an actor blue and photographing him under ultraviolet light, were dismissed outright by director Zack Snyder. Realizing the extent to which Billy Crudup – or just about any other actor, for that matter – would need to be altered to come close physically to the image of Dr. Manhattan in the graphic novel, Snyder opted instead for a fully CG character that would be heavily informed by Crudup's performance.

Ensuring that his performance was acquired and translated into the iconic blue man/deity was the job of VFX supervisor John DesJardin. "Creating Dr. Manhattan, first and foremost, is a leap of faith," he laughs. But that didn't mean that the other performers on the set should have to rely completely on their imaginations when acting opposite what would eventually become a purely digital image.

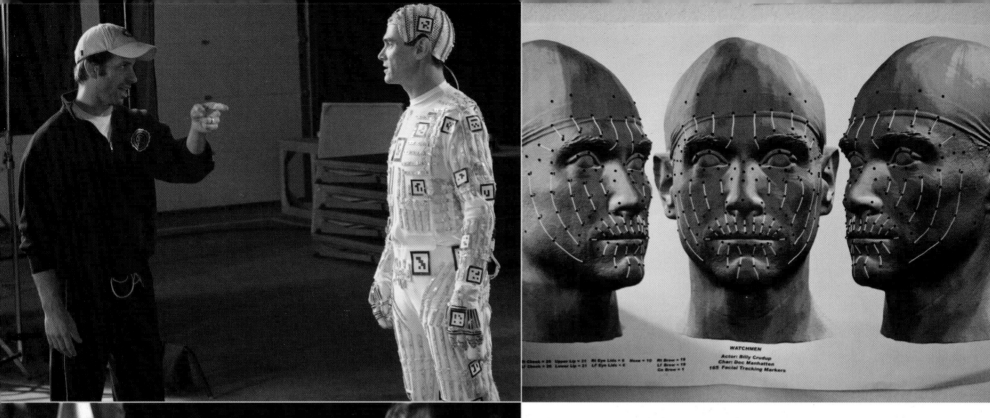

WATCHMEN
Actor: Billy Crudup
Char: Doc Manhattan
165 Facial Tracking Markers

Rt Cheek = 26   Upper Lip = 21   Rt Eye Lids = 6   Nose = 10   Rt Brow = 19
Lf Cheek = 26   Lower Lip = 21   Lf Eye Lids = 6   Lf Brow = 19
                                                                  Cn Brow = 1

"With CG characters in movies, with other actors around, you have to have some kind of a physical presence there," explains DesJardin. "It's not enough to put up a statue or a marionette, or say, 'Just do it all as a clean pass and we'll put him in later,' and have that kind of relationship exist in a vacuum. I don't think you can really do that. You need that presence for all the interaction and all the emotion."

That meant dressing and making up Crudup especially for a technique called "motion capture," often shortened to "mocap." "When we started out, we knew we needed a capture suit with rudimentary markers on it, just to get the body orientation," DesJardin points out. Hundreds of stenciled dots also covered Crudup's face at specific points. A high-resolution motion capture camera was then used to film all these points of reference, recording and storing the movements so they later could be applied to a 3-D model.

"He won't be unlike the [robot] character in *I, Robot* or the Silver Surfer [from *Fantastic Four: Rise of the Silver Surfer*], where we used the facial features and expressions with his voice," explains editor William Hoy, who cut both of those films. DesJardin recalls, "We took advantage of a lot of the development that Sony Imageworks has been undergoing for their performance capture, used a bit of foundation from what people were doing on *Pirates of the Caribbean* with Davy Jones, and amped it up a little bit for what we needed to do here."

Clockwise from opposite bottom: Director of Photography Larry Fong takes a reading on the light suit; Zack Snyder directs the super being before he lights up; casts of Billy Crudup's head, with reference points for facial expressions; Crudup prepares to master time and matter.

Previous spread: Jon Osterman goes to pieces.

This spread: Billy Crudup (above) provides the physical performance for Osterman's partially muscled skeleton (opposite).

Part of what needed to be "amped up" was Dr. Manhattan's body. "When Jon Osterman pulled himself back together, he made this ideal male form for himself to embody. He's really chiseled and he's gotta have that physicality to him," explains DesJardin. Bodybuilder Greg Plitt provided that physicality, which was digitally mapped to await transplanting and life-giving motion. "For lack of a better way of explaining it, we're taking Billy's head and we're putting it on the bodybuilder's body," says DesJardin, "and then Billy will provide the performance for that body as well as his own face."

DesJardin admits that keeping all those disparate elements in sync provided a unique challenge. "I've lost the one-to-one correspondence, and I have to somehow put the performance into this completely other body and being that's not the same size, and doesn't have any of the same characteristics, really." But he adds, "So far, it's been pretty astonishing how much we've been able to do and make it look right."

Dr. Manhattan, however, is not merely a statuesque, blue muscleman. He's a living embodiment of quantum physics. He's a source of power in his own right. "One of the big deals was not just can we have Billy do the performance on the set and track that performance," recalls DesJardin, "but can we get him to put out the other aspect of Dr. Manhattan that's really, really important – the fact that he glows blue all the time. Can we get that light into the scene? Can we get it onto the people he's with?"

DesJardin quickly rejected as being unnecessarily complicated the idea that the light be added during post-production. "Sure, we could build CG services in the room and light them up and track them to a character," he says, "but I thought, 'Why don't we try to get this in camera as much as we can?'" DesJardin realized that since they needed to have an actor in a capture suit already, that in itself could be used as the light source.

The earliest experiments in June, 2007 began with a black glove covered with blue LEDs, but the black absorbed too much of the light. "We needed a white glove with LEDs, because the white in the glove can help spread the light even further," explains DesJardin. "I tested that, and Zack and I looked at it, and the guys at Imageworks tracked their CG arm to that, and it all seemed to work." Warner Bros. approved a test suit, which DesJardin tried out at a studio in Marina Del Rey a month later. "We had a motion-capture actor wearing the suit. We did a little interaction with the set and my coordinator, Tricia Mulgrew. He went up to her and hugged her and she walked away, and we could see how all that interaction would play. And it really worked out well."

Jon Osterman is reborn as Dr. Manhattan in the Gila Flats cafeteria.

This spread: Elements, textures, and backgrounds are added, bit-by-bit, to create a convincing shot of Dr. Manhattan in his lab.

Next spread: Manhattan being blasted by Dr. Manhattan (or so the world believes).

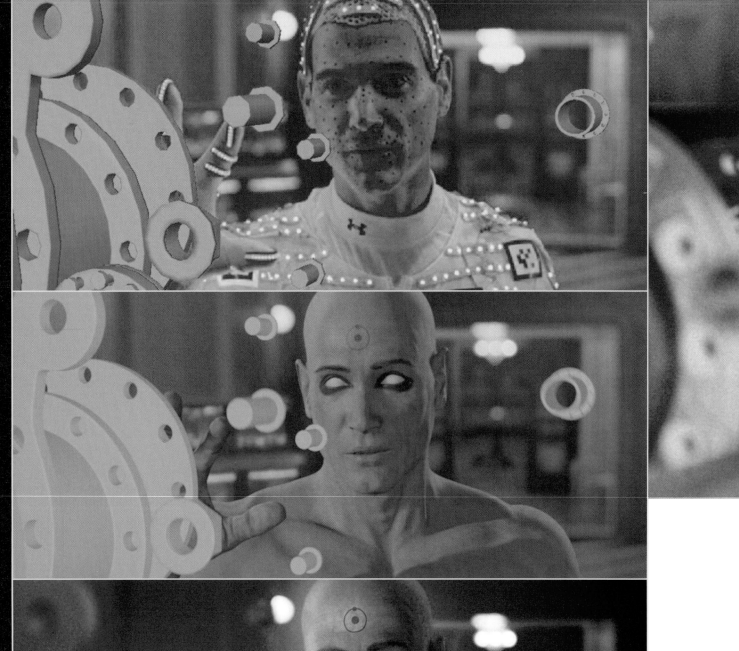

The final result was a complete bodysuit, including skullcap, covered in thousands of LEDs putting out a nice, diffuse, blue glow that touched everything around it. Crudup readily admits that the suit looked a bit goofy, and if anything, made getting into character that much more difficult. This was especially true when co-star Malin Akerman, playing his girlfriend, Laurie Juspeczyk, early on refused to take him seriously in the luminous outfit. "She stands there and laughs in my face for five out of seven days a week," recalls Crudup with a smirk, "and I'm supposed to be the master of all matter."

DesJardin worked in close collaboration with director of photography Larry Fong over several months to discover how best to utilize the light being given off. "I don't think we really figured it out totally until we got to Vancouver and started doing camera tests here," recalls DesJardin. "We narrowed it down to where we thought we knew how it was reacting so many feet from the light source." The LEDs were adjustable in terms of brilliance, and

DesJardin and Fong eventually determined that two settings were enough: a "normal" for indoor scenes and a "maximum" for shooting in full daylight.

Having Crudup in an illuminated suit produced other, unforeseen benefits. "Sometimes you want to light someone and give them eye light," says Fong. "Whenever Laurie, for example, talked to Dr. Manhattan, the glow from him produced all the sparkle in her eyes – it became more magical and did half the lighting for us sometimes. There are some scenes where he did all the lighting."

DesJardin is very happy with the final digital look of Dr. Manhattan, but is especially proud of the overall effect achieved by clothing the performer in light. "I look at everything around Billy, and I watch how it's hitting other objects, and I just keep thinking all the time, 'You'd never be able to back track that, make it up in post.' You can do a lot and nothing's impossible, but it would take a long, long time, and you get all this for free now, right? It's very inspiring."

"NOTHING EVER ENDS."
– DR. MANHATTAN

While the post crew was whittling down the final picture from 807,680 feet of film and putting the finishing touches on a modest 900+ VFX shots (*300*, by comparison, had about a third more despite its shorter run time), Zack Snyder and all of the principal actors, accompanied by Dave Gibbons, journeyed to San Diego in July to attend the annual Comic-Con International. A week earlier, a *Watchmen* teaser trailer had appeared at the head of *The Dark Knight*, giving a large segment of the movie-going public its first look at a different kind of super-hero film. Judging by the surge in sales of *Watchmen* graphic novels, it would appear that people were intrigued by what they saw.

At the *Watchmen* panel – arguably the most highly anticipated of the entire convention – they answered questions in front of some 6,500 die-hard fans that had waited in line for hours in the California sun for the opportunity. Snyder hemmed and hawed a bit like a politician when asked by an attendee in full Batman regalia who his favorite *Watchmen* character was (he eventually settled on "the girls"), but the crowd hung on every word uttered by the panelists. By the end of the event, their earnest responses and evident reverence for the source material had even the doubters admitting the project seemed to be in good hands. Snyder also screened an extended, R-rated trailer sans dialogue – twice, by popular demand – and the roar of positive response shook Hall H to the rafters.

There, at one of the vortexes of modern global popular culture, it makes one muse about the timing of *Watchmen*, and if it could be more perfect, for so many reasons. "We feel so lucky that Zack chose to do *Watchmen*," producer Larry Gordon says. "He lived up to the graphic novel's acclaim in every way, and having seen the film – it was well worth the wait."

Previous spread: New York takes a hit, as seen in pre-production art of the film's re-imagined ending by Dave Gibbons and colorist John Higgins.
Above: The many editions of *Watchmen*.

Clockwise from top: Dave Gibbons shows President Nixon reacting to strikes on multiple cities by "Dr. Manhattan"; Zack Snyder bathed in blue energy; another shot from the script's climax, as visualized by Gibbons.

Right: Laurie and Dan leave Veidt to mull over his actions.
Below: Walter Kovacs bears a prescient sign of the times.

From production designer Alex McDowell's point of view, the concepts of the graphic novel needed to age like a fine vintage before uncorking and savoring them. "This is exactly the right amount of time to have waited to make the film," he says. "If it had been made in 1987, it would've made no sense at all, with no perspective on the contemporary situation. But making it now, with the parallels that are going on – it's not a happy movie, but it's exactly the movie of our time. Although it's a period piece, it's an exact reference for now, this culture."

As for Snyder, he wholeheartedly agrees that the film is much more effective at commenting on the present by being set in the past. He also sees the recent spate of comic books coming to life on the big screen – some great and some not so great – as a positive environment for *Watchmen*'s release.

"The people who have grown up with super-hero movies, they're ready for super heroes to do something else," says Snyder. "It's like, 'Enough already. I get Spider-Man. I get Superman. I get Batman, for that matter, but I'm ready for them to do something *real*.' On top of that, you have anyone who's been alive in the 20th Century and observed pop culture. That person can also see in *Watchmen* the culmination of all of the pop ideas of the 20th Century finally intersecting at nuclear war and super heroes and fast food and fucking."

There's really no arguing with that statement.

Above: Electric vehicles herald a new era of guarded optimism.
Below left and right: Rorschach's journal holds the truth, and it's entirely in Seymour's hands.

Author's dedication

FOR MELISSA,
WHO MAKES THE WORLD AS FAR AS I'M CONCERNED.

Zack Snyder and the producers of *Watchmen* would like to extend a sincere thank you to all of the incredible artists, designers, photographers, actors, technicians and countless others who through their wealth of talent and tireless dedication helped to bring this film to life. It has been an amazing journey and we are incredibly grateful to have been able to share it with each and everyone of you. In addition, we would like to express our gratitude to everyone at Warner Bros., Paramount Pictures and Legendary Pictures.

Titan Books would like to thank Zack Snyder, Deborah Snyder, Larry Gordon, and Lloyd Levin for their enthusiastic co-operation, and especially Wes Coller, without whom this book would simply not have happened. Our thanks also go to Dave Gibbons for his support, and to the indefatigable John Morgan at DC Comics.

Peter Aperlo would also like to thank Eric Matthies for conducting and transcribing the vast majority of the interviews.

ACKNOWLEDGMENTS

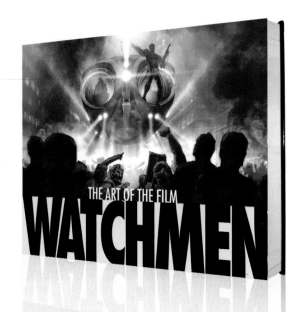
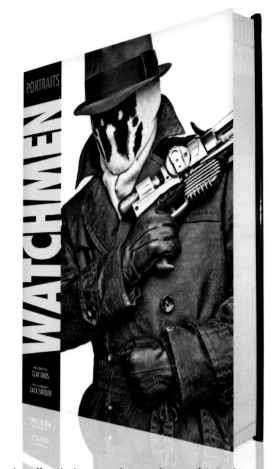